Management Sciences
Sciences
New Horizons

Management Sciences

New Horizons

Edited by Piotr Buła

Jagiellonian
University
Press

This publication was funded by the International Management Foundation

Reviewer
prof. dr hab. Szymon Cyfert

Publication coordination
Patryk Stawiarski

Cover design
Marta Jaszczuk

Cover photo
Jamesteohart (Adobe Stock)

ISBN 978-83-233-5350-8 (print)
ISBN 978-83-233-7537-1 (pdf)
ISBN 978-83-233-7538-8 (epub, mobi)
https://doi.org/10.4467/K7537.89/23.24.18678

JAGIELLONIAN
UNIVERSITY
PRESS

www.wuj.pl

Jagiellonian University Press
Editorial Offices: Michałowskiego 9/2, 31-126 Kraków
Phone: +48 12 663 23 80
Distribution: Phone: +48 12 631 01 97
Cell Phone: +48 506 006 674, e-mail: sprzedaz@wuj.pl
Bank: PEKAO SA, IBAN PL 80 1240 4722 1111 0000 4856 3325

Contents

Preface

The dynamics and scope of the changes taking place in the modern world force us to adapt quickly to the evolving environment. Individuals who excel at adapting to new realities gain an advantage in the global race to be better and more competitive. The source of such advantage is, first and foremost, the ability to anticipate the direction and nature of the changes shaping the emerging socio-economic order. This invaluable knowledge gives responsible and prudent managers the time to create adaptive and resilient organizations that can withstand structural disruptions.

To meet these needs, this publication brings together scholars and practitioners from various industries to address aspects of managing organizations in different sectors. It presents examples of how organizations have coped with the challenges of recent years, with a particular focus on the COVID-19 pandemic. In addition, it outlines key trends and phenomena that will intensify in the sectors studied in the future.

This publication is the result of an organized conference held on September 9–12 in 2022 in Sankt Gallen and Zurich, Switzerland This was the 11th foreign conference for Polish professors of organization and management sciences. The guiding theme of the conference was: Resilient Management in the New Era. At this point he would like to thank the two institutions hosting us: University of St. Gallen and the St. Gallen Integrated IMT Business School.

I would very much like to thank the organizers and institutions on the Polish side for their help and joint scientific debates. I would like to thank the members of the Committee on Organization and Management Sciences of the Polish Academy of Sciences, the staff of the Department of International Management at the Krakow University of Economics, Ms. President of the International Management Foundation for leading all formal matters, and the members and staff of the Prof. Jerzy Trzcieniecki Center.

I hope that as we stand at the threshold of a very pronounced technological revolution, we as managers and scientists will be able to demonstrate the foresight that will help make the world the one we all aspire to. I invite you to read this book towards new management sciences – new horizons. I hope that the book will be positively received from the readers.

Piotr Buła

CHRISTIAN ABEGGLEN, PH.D, ASSC. PROF.
Krakow University of Economics

PIOTR BUŁA, PH.D, ASSC. PROF.
Krakow University of Economics

CHRISTOPHER PAWLAK, PH.D.
Krakow University of Economics

Strategic capabilities management for supply chain in response to challenges in the global pharmaceutical industry

Abstract

The article comprises an analysis of key challenges and trends in the pharmaceutical sector and identifies the desired capabilities of pharmaceutical companies in the coming years. In this paper, the identified factors were grouped in the political, economic, sociocultural, technological, legal and environmental areas (PESTLE analysis) based on statistical and socioeconomic data, and the potential desired capabilities to be reinforced or developed by pharmaceutical companies in the next years were described.

Keywords: pharmaceutical industry, supply chain, operations, global trends, health system, biosimilars, artificial intelligence, generic pharmaceuticals, CMNN diseases, non-communicable diseases (NCDs), procurement, innovations, R&D, health expenditures, out-of-pocket health expenses

Introduction

Over the last 100 years, healthcare, which is part of the pharmaceutical industry, has been a continuously growing sector of the global economy. In recent decades, the development of pharmaceutical companies has remained relatively intact in regards to the global crisis, and the many challenges faced by the industry rather served as catalysts for further growth. The progress of innovative medicine was a driver for the entire business. This growth was protected by patent law, where the development of one drug would secure a pharmaceutical company for many years. The pharmaceutical industry, which is characterized by very long product life cycles, regulations, knowledge, intensive product developments and huge budgets, has created a unique environment where companies acquire unique sets of skills. However, in the face of current and future challenges, these skills might not be enough to remain competitive in long run. There are some unprecedented changes in the environment which will transform the supply chain, operations, and the way in which pharmaceutical companies will conduct their business.

The aim of this article is to analyze and segment the pharmaceutical sector's environment using the PESTLE method, resulting in a diagnosis and forecast of the dynamics, direction, nature and implications of changes that await this sector in the coming years. A better understanding of these changes is essential for elaborating strategies for the supply chain as well as the development of operational capabilities. In the first section, the authors attempted to identify key global challenges faced by the pharmaceutical industry as well as essential management capabilities for companies, with special attention to the practices in supply chain management.

Global trends in the pharmaceutical industry

Owing to the pharmaceutical industry, mankind has been able to treat the majority of health ailments, thereby saving millions of human beings and improving life expectancy. While this sector is known for profitability, stable growth, and resiliency to global economic turbulences, the current outlook is uncertain due to never before seen key trends, challenges and global shifts. Despite an aging population, the growing wealth of countries, and non-communicable diseases (NCDs), the industry is held back by global economic turbulences, pricing pressures from governments, and disruptive technological innovations popping up on horizon.

To prepare a framework for the study, the authors used PESTLE analysis. All identified key factors were summarized into political, economic, sociocultural, technological, legal, and environmental groups.

Political factors

"Pricing pressure", which is exerted by governments on pharmaceutical companies, is a key trend in the political sphere. Global expenditures as a percent of Gross Domestic Product are increasing. The highest dynamic is visible in the US and Canada, where the share of health expenditures has raised from 12.4% to almost 20% of the GPD (Figure 1). The second factor is the increasing share of governmental spendings in total health expenditures in the last 20 years (Figure 2). As out-of-pocket expenditures have no impact on state budgets, they are not a subject of governments' interest in the same way as governmental expenditures are, which leads to higher pricing pressure exerted on pharmaceutical companies by the government. This, in turn, will reduce medical reimbursement from governments, especially innovative reimbursement protected by patents. In the current, turbulent economic situation, the mere factor of pricing pressure might catalyze pricing pressure.

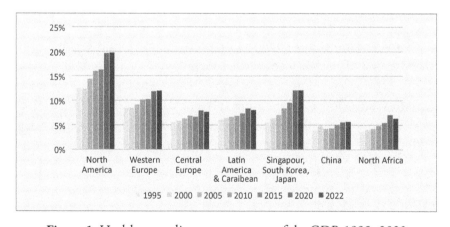

Figure 1. Health expenditures as a percent of the GDP, 1995–2022

Source: own elaboration based on data from University of Washington School of Medicine, the Institute for Health Metrics and Evaluation (IHME), January 3, 2023.

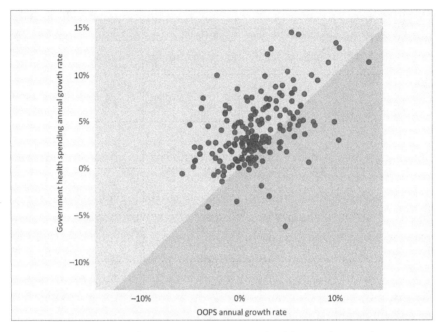

Figure 2. Growth of per capita government health spending and OOPS (out-of-pocket spending) in real terms, 2000–2020

Source: World Health Organization (2023, January 2), Global Heath Expenditure Database, https://apps.who.int/nha/database.

Some pharmaceutical companies, especially those whose revenue is generated mainly by innovative medicine, might find the pressure from governments very troublesome in the long term. These political factors in combination with the sociodemographic ones presented further in the article might catalyze the need to change business models, and will certainly require new skills in order to predict the economic aspects of innovations.

Economical factors

The economy is changing, and especially global economic turbulences will have a major impact on pharmaceutical companies. Multiple and complex factors impact the way in which pharmaceutical companies will need to organize supply chains and operations. The key trends include:

- R&D expenditure increase.
- Lower ROI from R&D investments.
- Higher efficiency pressure from generic companies.
- Higher failure rate of new drug developments.
- Upstream supply chain leading to more lost sales due to disruption of components' supply.

Higher R&D expenditures. The figures imply that the pharmaceutical industry spends the biggest % of revenue on R&D activities. While innovative pharmaceutical companies spend approx. 20–24% of their revenue on R&D, the computer software industry spends only 10.1% of it on R&D, the aerospace and military industry approx. 4.5%, the automotive industry – 4.4%, and the chemical industry only 2.6% of revenues (European Commission Report, 2015, p. 14).

Bringing a new drug to the market cost a pharmaceutical company around $2.7 billion in 2020 vs. approx. $1.2 billion in 2012 (Taylor et al., 2021). The same time risk of drug development failure is higher with only 2 in 10,000 drug molecules synthesized being patented and successfully passing all phases of clinical trials, while the success rate for all therapeutical area in the last two decades has been declining from 16.4% in 1999 (3-year average) to 11.6% for phase 1 in 2015 (Smietana, Siatkowski, and Møller, 2016). This has consequences in the form of a lower IRR (Internal Return Rate), which has declined from 6.4% in 2013 to 2.5% in 2020 (Taylor et al., 2021). It has even greater implications for the investment decisions of companies and investors. In recent decades, pharmaceutical companies were regarded by investors as a safe and profitable investment. However, the decline of IRR towards 2.5% will push investors in the direction of more lucrative areas of business, which could be an additional challenge for pharmaceutical companies to seek fundings for more risky and less profitable drug developments.

All of it will lead to the development of additional capabilities for much better financial engineering, risk management, and prediction modeling. Additionally, the identification of risk and better pipeline management will be desired capabilities for business case evaluation in order to decrease the ROI of the R&D innovation pipeline. Therefore, investment in the capabilities of prediction models based on AI or advance computing (quantum computers) might help to reduce the risk of failure, improving the ROI from R&D investment.

Higher spending on prescription drugs (both hospital and pharmacy distribution) represents only a fraction of total healthcare spending and amounted to $711 billion in 2011 (*Evaluate Pharm Report*, 2016, p. 10), representing merely 12% of total healthcare expenditures. OTC (over the counter) medicines account for approximately $45 billion of expenditure, bringing the total to around $756 billion per year for all medicines. In 2016, the spending on prescription drugs was $779 billion at factory prices according to the same report, and according to IMS[1] the largest company specializing in collecting data from the pharmaceutical market today spends $1.1 trillion at pharmacy prices (*Report – The Global Use of Medicines*, 2016, p. 6). This means that around one third of the value of medicines in pharmacies is consumed by their distribution. While distribution margins remain stable and exhibit a growing tendency, pharmaceutical companies might try to expand the supply chain downstream, developing their own channels (direct-to-pharmacies, direct-to-customer) or acquiring the existing ones.

Another factor is driven by COVID-19, which has temporarily slowed down the sales for a number of therapeutic areas (e.g., oncology) due to the suspension of other medical procedures such as cancer treatment. Hospital restrictions introduced in connection with the COVID-19 pandemic have already amounted to $1.265 trillion in 2020 (Figure 10), which equated to an average dynamic of 4.6% between 2016 and 2020. It must be noted that this dynamic, which equaled 7.4% (whereby the share of global expenditure increased to 23%) according to IQVIA Institute for Human Data Science (*Global Medicine Spending...*, 2021, p. 29), varies across developed countries and the so-called pharma-growing countries (*pharmerging*).

---

[1] The differences in sales volumes are mainly due to varying interpretations of medicines across countries, exchange rate differences and the so-called 'parallel export phenomenon', where medicines are re-exported to other countries where the price of the same medicine is more expensive. Poland, with some of the lowest drug prices, is significantly affected by this phenomenon.

Pressure from imitators (generic companies). A recent trend has been an increasing cost and innovation pressure from generic companies, i.e., ones that have not been considered innovative to date.

In recent years, the pharmaceutical market has been changing dynamically in terms of the share of innovators and generic companies. In the late 1940s, it was dominated by innovative pharmaceutical companies and this situation lasted until the 1980s. The last 30 years of regulatory changes have seen the emergence of a category of generic manufacturers according to WHO (2017).[2] These transformations have hit the innovators' business models and forced some of them to implement an imitation strategy as a complementary element (Sanofi, Novartis). Today, the share of generics is increasing. In the 1970s, generics accounted for less than a 5% share of total prescription drug sales, but already in 2016, according to the IMS Health Institute report they represented 45% of total prescription drug sales by pharmacy price in the entire industry (*Report – the Global Use of Medicines*, 2016, p. 2).

At the same time, the annual average growth in generic sales is almost 10%, with an around 5% growth in innovative medicines (patented drugs).

The share of generics in the sales volume of all pharmaceutical medicines varies significantly between countries (Figure 3). This is determined by a country's health and economic policies. For example, in countries with a large production capacity for innovative medicines, such as Belgium, Switzerland, or Ireland, the market share of generic companies is lower than in locations dominated by generic manufacturers. In countries where the pharmaceutical industry is not focused on the development of innovative medicines but has significant manufacturing capacity, generics account for a large share of the national market. A good example are countries of Central and Eastern Europe, which are dominated by generic medicines that are among the cheapest in Europe.

COVID-19 has served as a very vivid example and test of the innovative capabilities of many pharmaceutical companies. In late 2020, there were

---

[2] The revenue of generic pharmaceutical companies (*generics*) is generated mostly from the sale of drugs for which patent protection does not exist. *Originator* companies, on the other hand, profit mostly from the sale of drugs for which patent protection is still valid.

approx. 83 promising developments against Covid, many of which were re-lated to vaccines. It was obvious that the first company to launch the vaccine would acquire the biggest portion of demand. Indeed, in this "competition" innovative companies were likely to lose. This clearly shows that in innovation development, having merely a "molecule" is not enough. The entire process of commercialization (including clinical trials, production tests, quality val-idation, project management, etc.), and agile supply chains capable of cover-ing a large share of the demand very quickly, are winning. Therefore, pressure from generic companies does not merely involve pricing, there is also inno-vative pressure, especially in the area of operational excellence.

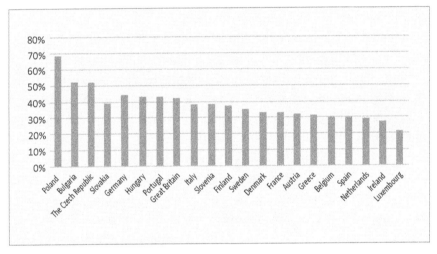

Figure 3. Percentage share of generics in the sales volume of all pharmaceutical drugs in 2010 (at pharmacy price)

Source: *Report on the Law on Reimbursement of Medicine: Implementation and Impact on Market Participants* (2011). London: IMS.

There is also a relation between the wealth of the state and the usage of generic medicine. Figure 3 illustrates the share of generics in the sale of all medicines in Europe in 2010. When the economy is more challenging, gener-ics are more prescribed more often. Pharmaceutical companies will sooner or later reach patents cliffs, where not too much will be left to discover. Therefore, this aspect of the pharmaceutical market will play a bigger and bigger role in the future, and there are at least two extreme scenarios. On one scale of the future landscape, most companies will become generics (cost efficiency will be critical), or on the other hand innovative companies will develop better, faster and overall cheaper solutions for health.

A turbulent supply chain as the new normal. In the last 50 years, the pharmaceutical supply chain has become global, very complex and in many cases – very lean. Due to economical turbulences, mainly inflation, currency fluctuation and demand volatility of therapeutical areas due to COVID-19, increase of energy cost, as well as shortages, wars including economic and trade wars, more difficulties in the supply of components are foreseen both in the short term horizon of 1–2 years but also in the longer period. Since 2020, the Global Supply Chain Pressure Index (GSCPI) has been reaching the biggest values, previously unseen in the last two decades (Figure 4), which will a have significant impact on supply interruptions as well as the availability of drugs.

Figure 4. Global Supply Chain Pressure Index, 1997–2022

Source: Federal Reserve Bank of New York, Global Supply Chain Pressure Index,

https://www.newyorkfed.org/research/gscpi.html.

Sociocultural factors

Another set of factors is related to demography and lifestyle changes, and will significantly impact the pharmaceutical industry in the coming years. Also, the increasingly complex and restrictive regulation of drug quality and safety is resulting in ever higher costs for new development, production, and distribution.

It is widely accepted in the pharmaceutical sector that the market is divided into geographical areas, considering the purchasing power in each country. Pharmaceutically developed locations include the US, Canada, Japan, South Korea and the five main European Union countries. However, due to demographic changes, the share of developed countries in total global consumptions has declined to approximately 57% in 2016 from 73% in 2006. This trend is set to continue over the coming years. The US share of global sales fell from 41% in 2006 to 31% in 2016, and the spending share of the main EU countries (Germany, UK, France, Italy, Spain) dropped to 13% in 2016 (*Report – the Global Use of Medicines*, 2016).

While the overall global structure remains the same, the APAC region will become a bigger market for global health.

The expenditure by pharmaceutical markets (*pharmerging*)[3] has exceeded that of the so-called Big 5 (EU5) and amounted to 30% of global expenditure in 2016, mainly due to greater access to healthcare (with tens of millions of people in China) and the increasing purchasing power of their populations (Figure 11). As a result, the growth rate of total health expenditure is expected to increase further, averaging 6.7% per annum between 2014 and 2018, which is higher than Europe.

The main drivers of growth in drug expenditure are:

◆ development of specialized therapies in developed markets,[4]
◆ improving health services and growing wealth of densely populated countries, and thus better access to medicines (China, Russia, India, Brazil, Chile, Algeria, Bangladesh, and the Philippines),

---

[3] Emerging countries include China, Brazil, India, Russia, Mexico, Turkey, Poland, Venezuela, Argentina, Indonesia, South Africa, Thailand, Romania, Egypt, Ukraine, Pakistan, and Vietnam.

[4] US, Japan, Germany, France, Italy, Spain, UK, Canada, South Korea. The IMS predicts that approx. 225 new medicines will be launched by 2020, which is almost

◆ population ageing in developed countries,
◆ changes in lifestyle in developing regions.

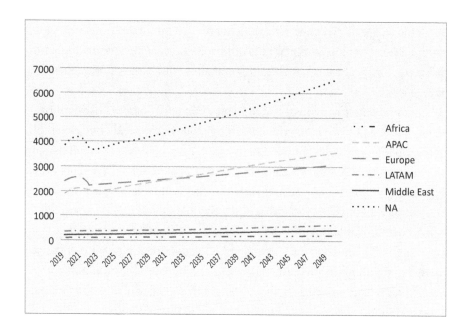

Figure 5. Global Expected Health Spending in USD, 2019–2049 (in millions)

Source: own elaboration based on the *Global Burden of Disease Collaborative Network.*
Global Expected Health Spending 2019–2050 (2021). Seattle: Institute for Health
Metrics and Evaluation (IHME).

The above figures also consider factors that lead to a deceleration in the growth of the pharmaceutical market. The main factors include the expiry

20% more (184) than were authorized between 2011 and 2015. New technologies and methods of developing medicines for diseases previously difficult to treat such as cancer, dermatology, immunology, diabetes, diseases of the nervous system typical of old age: sclerosis, Alzheimer's, Parkinson's, etc., will be introduced. The higher volume of drugs is the result of falling average total revenues associated with the entire cycle of patent protection. Rare diseases, affecting fewer patients, mean that the rate of return on drug R&D costs will fall (Figure 8).

of patent protection, which reduces the value of the pharmaceutical market. The magnitude of this factor is estimated to be around $178 billion per year between 2015 and 2020 (which represents around 12% of the size of the total pharmaceutical market).

This will lead pharmaceutical companies to move their business closer to the faster growing markets. For supply chain, it means mainly higher capabilities for localization, technology transfers, and external manufacturing management.

Another factor involves the lifestyle change of society. The economic development of poor countries has brought with it typical civilization diseases (obesity, stress, less physical activities etc.), which had led to dominant burdens on health systems, and the greatest causes of healthy years of life lost. The combination of various factors reduces the relative impact of communicable, maternal, neonatal, and nutritional (CMNN) diseases,[5] while non-communicable diseases (NCDs)[6] have risen in relative prevalence (Figure 6) globally. The dynamic growth of NCDs is encountered also in the fast growing region of South-East Asia, while the European region remains relatively stable due to a higher awareness regarding health, as well as a better health system.

The fastest annual growth rates between 2021 and 2025 are to be expected in the so-called Pharmerging countries, namely China: 4.5–7.5% and Russia: 11–14%. For the same period of time, growth in developed countries is estimated at minus 0.1 – plus 0.4%.

---

[5]   CMNN diseases (Communicable, maternal, neonatal, and nutritional diseases) are typical conditions caused by viruses, bacteria, fungus, and protozoa. The top 10 diseases are: Malaria, Methicillin-resistant Staphylococcus aureus, Pertussis, Rabies, Sexually Transmitted Disease (HIV), Shigellosis, Tuberculosis, West Nile Virus, Zika.

[6]   Non-communicable diseases are not spread through infection or other people but are typically caused by unhealthy behaviors. They are the leading cause of death worldwide and present a huge threat to health and development, particularly in low- and middle-income countries. The top 10 typical diseases are: Alzheimer's, Cancer, Epilepsy, Osteoarthritis, Osteoporosis, Cerebrovascular Disease (Stroke), Chronic Obstructive Pulmonary Disease (COPD), Coronary Artery Disease.

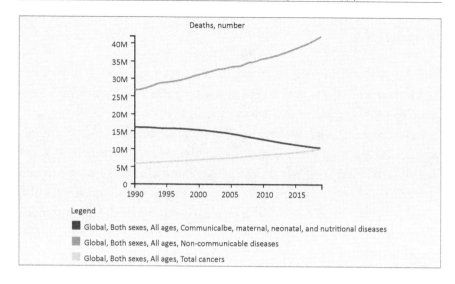

Figure 6. Death driven by non-communicable diseases and CMNN diseases, 1995–2020

Source: own elaboration based on data acquired from *United States Health Care Spending by Payer and Health Condition 1996–2016* (2020). Seattle: Institute for Health Metrics and Evaluation (IHME).

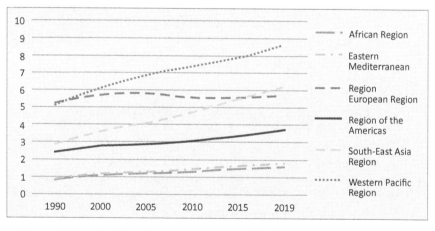

Figure 7. Death driven by non-communicable diseases per WHO regions, 1995–2020

Source: own development based on data acquired from *United States Health Care Spending by Payer and Health Condition 1996–2016* (2020). Seattle, United States of America: Institute for Health Metrics and Evaluation (IHME).

Technological factors

There are many technological factors on rise which will severely impact various industries in the next year. The pharmaceutical sector follows the same trend too as other industries. Among which key trends are following: artificial intelligence, machine learning, 3D printing, IoT (internet-of-things) advanced computing technologies, and digitalization (blockchain, eCloud, Real-World Data, Big-Data Analytics, advanced analytics and prediction models, remote diagnostics), precision medicine, There is currently also a heated debate about biological technologies (immunotherapies, genetic engineering, bioprinting), which will have a broad and common impact on new therapeutical areas.

Artificial intelligence and advanced computing will affect diagnosis (example: pharma giant Bayer has strengthened its ties with healthcare technology company Huma to develop an AI model that can identify and distinguish the characteristics of different types of lung cancers according to Andrea Park (2021)) and drug development in terms of molecular modelling and predictive analysis in order to increase the probability of success and reduce the time-to-market. Digitalization also can increase the speed of clinical trials by reducing the time of data collection for each phase of trials. Finally, advance computing and AI can significantly help in the supply chain in predictive modeling for planning.

Table 1. Artificial Intelligence and Digital Transformation

Area	Application
Design and monitoring of clinical trials	• Patient dropout • Monitoring of trials • Subject enrolment/selection • **Bioprinting** (3D), creating imitations of natural human tissue and organs for testing drug toxicity, specific dosage, metabolism measurement, etc.

Area	Application
Manufacturing	• Identification of critical quality manufacturing process parameters (**IoT**) • Navigating future production cycles (**Predictive models**) • Prediction of malfunction on production lines (**IoT, predictive models**) • Automated manufacturing (**machine learning**) • Customized manufacturing (**3D printing**)
Planning & Supply	• Market demand prediction and more accurate planning (**Digitalization, Real-Data World**) • Better inventory level (less stock-outs) (**Real-Data World, Digitalization, Big Data Analytics**) • Improved prediction of supply chain interruption (**Real-World data, Big Data Analytics**) • Improved traceability of shipments (**blockchain**)
Drug discovery	• Drug design (Protein structure prediction, Protein interaction) – **Advanced computing and AI** • Drug Screening (Bioactivity prediction, Physic-chemical parameters prediction) – **Advanced computing and AI**

Source: own elaboration.

Another area involves the advancement of biotechnology and availably of biosimilars, which will change the structure of the manufacturing landscape, demand for skilled workers, and need for capital investments,[7] with more dynamic growth expected for biotechnology drugs (especially in the area of immunotherapy), which are among the most innovative and effective man-made medicines currently available (Table 2).

---

[7] Due to a very capital intensive manufacturing process involving stringent quality standards, it might also create a need of collaboration between current competitors or an explosion of the external manufacturing footprint.

Table 2. Current and projected sales volumes of conventional and biotech medicines from 2008 to 2022 at factory prices with a division of medicines into conventional and biotech

Drug group	2012	2013	2014	2015	2016	2017	2018	2019	2020	2021	2022	2023	2024
Biotech-nology	152	165	178	184	200	220	242	266	290	320	350	370	425
Conven-tional	440	431	442	433	440	453	473	497	527	514	518	542	532
Other	161	166	168	159	171	185	196	207	220	225	231	237	241
Total sales	**754**	**762**	**788**	**776**	**812**	**858**	**911**	**970**	**1037**	**1059**	**1099**	**1149**	**1198**

Source: own compilation based on the *Evaluate Pharm Report: World Preview 2016. Outlook 2022* (2016). 9th Edition. London: Statista and IMS, 20.

It is expected that biotechnologies and especially biosimilars, which will comprise similar copies of original biotech drugs, will serve as a powerful source of savings for governmental budgets and at the same time a major source of revenue for generic companies (Figure 8). At the same time, conventional medicine based on chemical synthesis will be declining and is bound to be replaced by biotechnological medicine. The growth of biosimilars in the next 10 years is estimated at approx. 23–25% CAGR, while that of the entire pharmaceutical industry CAGR will be approx. 6%.

The pharmaceutical industry is characterized by a very strict and deep regulatory framework. Almost every operational aspect of pharmaceutical companies is strictly regulated. Huge numbers of government and non-government agencies supervise, control and define the operating practices within the pharmaceutical industry. In most cases, this is linked to the safety of medications (in terms of development and quality) as well as ethical behaviors (strict regulations for advertisement and sales activities).

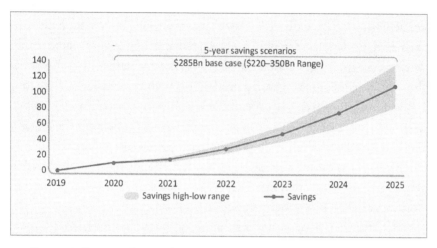

Figure 8. Estimated costs due to popularization of biosimilar medicines between 2019 and 2025

Source: *Global Medicine Spending and Usage Trends: Outlook to 2025* (2021). Parsippany: IQVIA Institute for Human Data Science, p. 35.

In all cases, this stringent and complex regulatory framework comprises a serious barrier for small companies (such as start-ups and other potential competitors incl. non-pharma competitors like Amazon, Samsung etc.) to enter the pharmaceutical industry, which could imply that established drug manufacturers and distributors have a much easier situation.

At the same time, the drug development process is time-consuming and takes between 6 and 15 years, with an average of 12 to 13 years (*The Pharmaceutical Industry in Figures*, 2016, p. 5). Assuming that patent protection lasts 20 years, the speed with which innovations reach the market will be particularly important for market success, as was the case for Pfizer, which is the dominant manufacturer of the COVID-19 vaccine, estimated to have a market share of around 65% and a vaccine revenue growth of $7.8 billion in Q2 2021 alone (revenue growth of almost 20%).

Also, growing numbers of complex regulations over the globe incl. the atomization of regional regulations has led to an enormous increase of complexity within the supply chain, and therefore cost increase (smaller production lots, more costly changes of specifications); this is counterproductive to cost efficiency. In practice, it means that many countries are implementing their own regulations related to claims, ingredients, and quality requirements. This leads to increased numbers of health-related regulatory inspections and more strict regulations regarding production environment control, creating a need for additional capital expenditures (aggregation, serialization, temperature control, temper evidence in packaging). Another factor is the requirement of localization of production in many countries (mainly the middle east), which has caused a situation in which medicine must be produced in the country of sales, otherwise sales are not possible, or it will have an economic impact on profitability due custom tariffs.

One particular consequence of more strict regulations and additional requirements in drug development is the increased length of clinical trials (Figure 9).

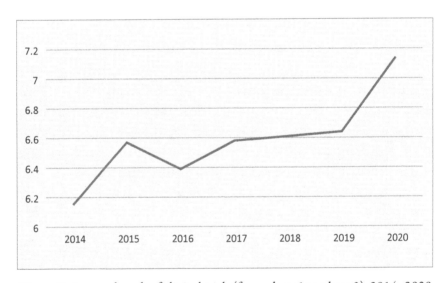

Figure 9. Average length of clinical trials (from phase 1 to phase 3), 2014–2020

Source: Taylor K., Shah S., Curz M., Wendell M. (2021). *Seed of Changes: Measuring the Return from Pharmaceutical Innovation*. London: Deloitte Center for Health Solutions.

Environmental factors

Environmental factors are mainly related to climate change, increased pollution (air, water, food), degeneration of the natural environment, and intensified human-animal contacts, which lead to: the spread of sickness (obesity, diabetics, less nutrients in food), a weaker immune system of human beings, and higher risk of epidemics, with faster outbreak in the "global village", increase of oncological sickness, increase of AMR[8] and allergies.

All of the above are changing the structure of spending on therapeutic areas. Specifically, the largest increases between 2021 and 2025 are expected in oncology (9–12%), immunotherapy (9–12%), diabetes (4–7%), and vaccines (12–15%) (Figure 10).

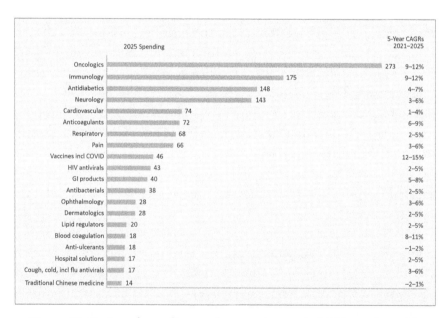

Figure 10. Projected spending on therapeutic areas in 2025 together with the average rate of growth in spending between 2021 and 2025 (USD)

Source: *Global Medicine Spending and Usage Trends: Outlook to 2025* (2021). Parsippany: IQVIA Institute for Human Data Science, p. 39.

---

[8]   Antimicrobe resistance diseases.

All of the key trends and challenges mentioned above will require pharmaceutical companies to adapt. Some might find this to be a challenge, and companies that adopt faster will gain competitive edge. For many pharmaceutical businesses, the last decades were relatively stable. A high margin failed to trigger big restructuring programs, a long product life cycle (covered by patents protection) has led to a situation in which management practices and operational capabilities remain relatively unchanged in comparison to other companies operating on in a much more aggressive and competitive environment on a daily basis, which has forced them to be operationally fit and agile. Therefore, understanding the key trends and their consequences might be critical in the development of new capabilities in regards with operations and the supply chain.

Pharmaceutical companies are facing turbulence, thereby acquisitions and mergers will be very dynamic. The former will be used by pharmaceutical companies to reduce production and distribution costs, as well as to develop new innovative drugs. In addition, acquisitions and takeovers are fueled by increasing technological and quality requirements, as well as high pressure exerted by regulators and payers (lowering budgets), which translates into greater pressure to improve cost efficiency. Through acquisitions and market consolidation, the costs of sourcing raw materials and distributing finished drugs (especially in the so-called "cold supply chain") are being reduced. As far as acquisitions are concerned, it will require better capabilities for business due diligence, process standardization, and technology transfer.

The main objective of any enterprise is to generate profit and continuously improve its competitiveness. The main researchers of innovation (Porter, 1998; Hamel and Prahalad, 1994; Kay, 1993), believe that the ability to create and use innovation is one of the most important factors in building competitive edge in business. This statement is especially valid for pharmaceutical industry. Therefore, it is worth to stay focused on the capabilities of innovations management. A company's innovativeness should be strategic and managed accordingly. The goal for proper planning is to define an innovation strategy, several definitions of which are approximated below.

Considering the challenges described in the PESTLE analysis (pressure from generic companies, an "expiry" of patents in the long run will lead to the effect of patent cliff), it is important to take note of the opportunities brought by innovation strategy management and to focus on the product life cycle according to Dietl (1985), i.e., introducing new products to international markets. Innovation strategy can be understood as a plan to guide a new product through the competitive struggle (Bogdanienko, 2008). It therefore involves several different functions that will support a product launch. The supply chain can play an important role in securing capacity (fast supply growth-to-market) from its component suppliers, lowering the cost of the marketed innovation (cost-to-market), and bringing the product quickly to the market (time-to-market).

Innovation concepts define how innovation should be used to achieve a competitive advantage (Gilbert, 1994). The integration of innovation strategy into the overall company policy is intended to lay the foundations for the future position of the enterprise in the market and to identify the core of the company's competitive edge.

From the perspective of a company that finds itself among other players in the market, two types of attitudes towards innovation strategy can be distinguished according to Kosińska (2008):

An attitude of innovative leadership – involving the creation of the market through a continuous and systematic introduction of novelties to it.

An attitude of imitation – a strategy for responding to the innovator's actions.

An innovation leadership strategy will focus on evolutionary innovation or disruptive innovation. It depends on the ability to combine cutting-edge technology with the adaptability of the changing market or customer needs, all while avoiding formality (Morgan, 2010).

The strategy should consider global competition mechanisms and shape the competitiveness of organizations based not only on innovation trends in the areas of product, but also pay special attention to process improvement, organizational innovation and finally overall process excellence. In practice, this implies the need to move away from the traditional model of competition towards a competition strategy based on innovation and excellence.

As regarding strategy development, here attention is focused on the business environment of the enterprise, and the most salient features of an innovation strategy are: the formulation of an innovation portfolio correlated with the long-term strategy, consideration of the strategic area, alignment of the research project portfolio with market needs and opportunities (licensing, patenting, continuing education), integration of development and business strategies, and a continuous partnership and cross-functional collaboration capabilities between research, production and business personnel in relations inside and outside the enterprise (Marek and Białasiewicz, 2011).

Therefore, an innovation strategy cannot be limited only to R&D factors for new products or merely defining a plan. A part of the scheme should also set out the internal aspects of the company; it should be a way of looking at the whole organization through the prism of its external activities and internal resources.[9]

Given the relatively intensive growth of specific therapeutical areas (oncology, immunotherapy, etc.) and new technologies (biomedicine), there will be a need to develop the following capabilities depending on types of innovation, as well as considering the innovation factors, target and desired timing of implementation (Table 3).

The choice of innovation strategy has a strong impact on functional strategies. Here, a company's vision can define the strategies of its functional departments (marketing, R&D, personnel management, supply chain, purchasing, etc.).

However, sometimes despite the proven impact of innovation in shaping competitive advantage, innovation is not a commonly developed capability of a company to build competitive edge (Plawgo and Kornecki, 2010).

---

[9]   Based on the above discussion, the following definition of innovation strategy is adopted in the PhD: "It is finding the most optimal way to exploit, develop internal resources, search for and create opportunities in the market in the long term in order to gain competitive advantage through the targeted and organized introduction of innovations to the market. Innovation strategy is also the management of the existing product portfolio and life cycle in order to maximize profitability in the short and long term, and to develop innovation internally."

Table 3. Capabilities and innovation strategy types

Classification criteria	Types innovation strategy	Desired capabilities (brief description)
Innovation factors	R&D	Collaboration with academic and external institutions in joint development, including CDMOs. This includes innovation proposals, evaluation of ideas (filtering, evaluation, feedback).
	Purchase of licenses	Purchase of domestic and foreign licenses from external partners (suppliers, CMOs).
	Own concepts	Shortening the innovation development cycle. Also called the time-to-market, which is related to process excellence for validation, technology transfer activities, or production scale-up efficiency.
Time to implement innovations	Pioneering	Going beyond product innovation, in pioneering, important capabilities are related to cost-to-market. This means design-to-value and supply chain design. Fast and efficient closure of manufacturing technology gaps.
	Imitative	Innovative companies might respond by developing a cheaper version of an innovation or by implementing it faster.

Source: prepared by the authors.

Conclusion

The development of capabilities in response to global challenges identified in the PESTLE analysis will depend on the nature and business strategy of pharmaceutical companies. Proper management of capabilities will serve as a critical success factor for a smooth and effective implementation of strategies as an answer to global trends. Organizations should therefore manage this process in a structured and cautious manner; therefore, the management of capabilities should be part of regular strategic processes.

While there are various favorable components such as growth in purchasing power and technological innovations, constituents like strict regulations, a health-conscious lifestyle and sociocultural factors could be the case of downfall. In the wake of this fact, a new set of capabilities in supply chain and operations will be essential to hold competitive advantage summarized in the below table (Table 4).

Table 4. PESTLE analysis and an example of the desired capabilities within supply chain and operations for pharmaceutical companies in the coming years

Area	Key Trend	Capabilities
Political	• Decline of governmental reimbursement for patented drugs • Pricing pressure from governments	• Design-to-value in order to develop cost efficient medicine • Proactive design of supply chains in order to develop more stable and cost-efficient end-to-end supply chains • Total cost of ownership

Area	Key Trend	Capabilities
Economical	• Increase of R&D expenditures • Lower IRR from R&D investments • Higher economic efficiency pressure from generic companies • Higher failure rate of new drug developments • Lost revenue due to patents expiry (patent cliff) • Higher inflation in the upstream supply chain • More volatile demand and supply of components (more disruptions in supply)	• Time-to-market capabilities (technology transfers) to gain better IRR from patented medicine • Digitalization, advance computing, and AI (predicative analysis) to increase the success rate of developed medicine • Big data analytics for better supply chain planning to offset more volatile demand fluctuations • Real-World Data in response to a more fluctuating demand and early identification of supply disruption • Fast capacity development (agile supply chains) • Innovation sourcing • Increased safety stocks, dual sourcing, technology transfer • Improved business due diligence to monitor the risk of insolvency • Crisis & supply interruption management • Suppliers and supply chain risk management (dual sourcing, data collection and monitoring)

Area	Key Trend	Capabilities
Sociocultural	• Changes in lifestyle • Aging population • Increased spending in emerging countries • Increased influence of non-governmental organizations • NCDs' increase in developing countries	• Faster technology transfers from region to another • Higher external manufacturing to develop production in proximity to the market • Improved Corporate Social Responsibility skills
Legal	• More demanding regulations • Longer clinical trials • Atomization of global regulations	• Time-to-market of clinical trials to offset longer clinical trials • Product customization (Operational Excellence in Manufacturing) • Smart portfolio management • Short, customized production campaigns • Manufacturing excellence (OEE, SMED) • More transparent and standardized quality management
Environmental	• Dynamic changes in structure of therapeutic areas to NC • More pandemics	• More agile supply chains (External manufacturing) to respond faster to market needs • Better market scanning (procurement search capabilities) • Virtual team management, talent management in the supply chain due to the global manufacturing footprint

Source: prepared by the authors.

Finally, the authors firmly believe that the management of capabilities is an extremely important subject for companies facing global trends, and the scope of topics is much beyond the content of this article. Therefore, the main intension of this paper was to inspire the academic world to conduct more in-depth research in this area.

References

Bogdanienko J. (2008). *In Pursuit of Modernity: Selected Aspects of Creating and Implementing Change.* Toruń: Scientific Society of Organisation and Management.

Buła P. (ed.) (2010). *Contemporary Problems of Entrepreneurship in Small and Medium-Sized Enterprises.* Cracow: Cracow Business School of the Cracow University of Economics.

Dietl J. (1985). *Marketing.* Warszawa: PWE.

Drucker P.F. (2004). "Dyscyplina w podejściu do innowacji". *Harvard Business Review Polska* 1.

European Commission Report, *Industry R&D Expenditure Scoreboard 2015.* EU 2015.

Evaluate Pharm Report: World Preview 2016, Outlook to 2022 (2016). 9th Edition. London: Statista and IMS.

Gilbert T.J (1994). "Choosing an innovation strategy: Theory and practice". *Business Horizons* 37(6), 16–22.

Global Burden of Disease Collaborative Network. Global Expected Health Spending 2019–2050 (2021). Seattle: Institute for Health Metrics and Evaluation (IHME).

Global Medicine Spending and Usage Trends: Outlook to 2025 (2021). Parsippany: IQVIA Institute for Human Data Science.

Hamel G. and Prahalad C.K. (1994). *Competing for the Future.* Cambridge, Massachusetts: Harvard Business School Press.

Janasz K. (2011). "Innovation decisions in the enterprise". *Zeszyty Naukowe Uniwersytetu Szczecińskiego* 639. *Finanse, Rynki Finansowe, Ubezpieczenia* 37, 830–841.

Kay J. (1993). *The Foundations of Corporate Success.* Oxford: Oxford University Press.

Kosińska E. (ed.) (2008). *Marketing międzynarodowy. Zarys problematyki.* Warszawa: PWE.

Leśniak-Łebkowska G. (2014). "Zarządzanie proinnowacyjne w warunkach nietrwałych przewag konkurencyjnych". *Studia Ekonomiczne* 183(1), 162–174.

Leśniak-Łebkowska G. (2003). "Doskonałość operacyjna i zarządzanie ryzykiem, jako podstawy sukcesu strategicznego przedsiębiorstwa". *Zarządzanie i Finanse* 4(2), 191–201.

Marek S. and Białasiewicz M. (ed.) (2011). *Podstawy nauki o organizacji. Enterprise as an economic organization*. Warszawa: PWE.

McGrath R.G. (2013). "Transient advantage". *Harvard Business Review* 91(6), 62–70.

Morgan M. (2010). *Effective Implementation of Strategy*. Warszawa: Scientific Publishers PWN.

Park A. (2021). *Bayer strengthens ties with Huma, collaborating on AI to classify lung cancer types*. Fierce Biotech. https://www.fiercebiotech.com/medtech/bayer-strengthens-ties-huma-collaborating-ai-to-classify-lung-cancer-types. Accessed: 27.12.2022.

The Pharmaceutical Industry in Figures: Key Data (2016). Brussels: The European Federation of Pharmaceutical Industries and Associations.

Plawgo B. and Kornecki J. (2010). *Wykształcenie pracowników a pozycja konkurencyjna przedsiębiorstwa*. Warszawa: Polska Agencja Rozwoju Przedsiębiorczości.

Porter M.E. (1998). *Competitive Advantage: Creating and Sustaining Superior Performance*. New York: Free Press.

Report on the Law on Reimbursement of Medicine: Implementation and Impact on Market Participants (2011). London: IMS.

Report – the Global Use of Medicines: Outlook Through 2016 (2016). London: IMS Institute for Healthcare Informatics.

Smietana K., Siatkowski M. and Møller M. (2016). "Trends in clinical success rates". *Nat Rev Drug Discovery* 15(6), 379–380. https://doi.org/10.1038/nrd.2016.85.

Taylor K., Shah S., Curz M., Wendell M. (2021). *Seed of Changes: Measuring the Return from Pharmaceutical Innovation*. London: Deloitte Center for Health Solutions.

Twiss B. (1986). *Managing Technological Innovations*. London: Longman Publishing Group.

United States Health Care Spending by Payer and Health Condition 1996–2016 (2020). Seattle: Institute for Health Metrics and Evaluation (IHME).

LESZEK BOHDANOWICZ, PH.D, ASSC. PROF.
University of Lodz

The impact of the coronavirus pandemic on the management of football clubs: The case of Widzew Łódź in the 2020/2021 season

Abstract

The spread of COVID-19, which began in earnest in 2020, has hit enterprises across many industries by influencing their financial results and operations. Sectors particularly exposed to the consequences were involved in the organization of mass events, including sports events. This article addresses the problems of football clubs in Poland and around the world caused by this pandemic. The paper aims to present the coronavirus' impact on the management of football clubs on the example of the Polish professional football club Widzew Łódź. Firstly, the article describes problems in the functioning of European and Polish football clubs during COVID-19 while the further section elaborates on Widzew Łódź and the impact of COVID-19 on management and sports activities.

Keywords: football clubs management, strategic management, value management, coronavirus pandemic, fan engagement

Introduction

The beginning of 2020 has brought a severe threat to the functioning of enterprises all over the world. The coronavirus pandemic has affected many companies from various sectors. It was of particular importance for industries dealing with managing clients' free time, including the organization of mass events, such as cinemas, theatres, restaurants, entertainment, and sports.

This last area has experienced something unprecedented. It is enough to mention that huge events were postponed to the following year, and this includes the Olympic Games in Tokyo, the European Football Championship (Euro 2020) for the first time in eleven countries (counting England and Scotland separately), and the South American Football Championship (Copa America 2020). All competitions were postponed. Although the pandemic is not over, the costs incurred by the organizers meant that the planned events, regardless of the possibility of suffering losses, were held only in 2021. In this case, it was necessary to continue the sports competition.

Polish football authorities have also suspended national football games. The clubs were unsure if they would continue games. This problematic situation was faced by the top management, which counted economic losses and was constantly struggling to maintain financial liquidity. The subsequent suspension of matches due to the lack of an audience, and then with a limited number of spectators, also did not significantly improve the situation of football clubs (in American English soccer clubs), also in Poland.

This article discusses the functioning of football clubs during the pandemic in the spring of 2020. It also serves as a good illustration of how unpredictable environmental changes can affect organizations from the entertainment and sport industry. The purpose is to present the impact of COVID-19 on the management of football clubs in the 2019/2020 season. Besides demonstrating the general situation of professional football clubs in the world, we elaborate on the organizational and sports context of the Polish league on the example of the Widzew Łódź football club.

Football clubs as business organizations

Since the early 1990s, football clubs have undergone significant changes. The methods of management have been subject to major transformations, and it has been openly declared that they should be addressed in a similar way to business enterprises. On the one hand, they are designed to generate financial results, while on the other, sports outcomes are of crucial importance for their evaluation. If a club cannot achieve a set sports result, in which case it negatively affects the generated revenues, and it may even spiral into bank-ruptcy (Kuper and Szymański, 2019; Rohde and Breuer, 2017).

Nevertheless, football clubs are guided by a different philosophy of oper-ation, in which two systems, business and sports, function side by side. The latter usually has an advantage over the former. The key to sports competi-tion is not profit, but the desire to win, high ambitions, and the aspiration to achieve success. By appealing to the nature of the sport, football fans exert pressure on the authorities. They are often focused on the sporting outcome, even at the expense of the economic effect. As a result, club authorities over-estimate income items and experience difficulties in maintaining the level of costs and achieving budgetary goals. The latter can even be deliberately abandoned when an opportunity presents itself to earn a good sports result. There is no guarantee that the club will repeat it in the next season, especial-ly when its sports and financial potential is close to that of the competitors.

At the same time, clubs with a poorer financial potential may find it chal-lenging to maintain their league status in the future. Hence most clubs at-tempt to compete on the sports level and increase their expenses. A non-com-peting club will lower its position. Therefore, as a rational measure it should reinvest positive financial results in sports activities. Thus, if a club wishes to remain at the forefront of the league for a more extended period, then its po-tential profit will be diminished by rising costs. The problem is compounded by the fact that relatively small differences in football performance through-out a season are often associated with significant differences in income. Fur-thermore, an increase in income inequality creates a system of incentives to motivate football clubs to behave in a gambling-like manner. This mode of operation is particularly exposed upon the occurrence of unforeseen turbu-lences in the environment, such as the COVID-19 pandemic.

Revenue is generated by football clubs from a variety of sources. Tradi-tional sources involved tickets, including seasonal tickets and catering served during games. Today, however, clubs play at modern stadiums, which differ-entiate prices for watching sports competitions and performing hospitali-ty services. The wealthier fans can watch matches from company skyboxes or selected locations, and can use other services, such as meals and alcohol. But these are not all the possibilities of football clubs. Football clubs have also significantly increased their revenues thanks to intensified sponsorship and television broadcasts. Merchandising is yet another source. The sale of t-shirts, souvenirs, and a wide range of gadgets provides more and more opportunities due to the development of e-commerce.

Football clubs conduct sales in stationary and online stores. Another primary source of revenue are sponsors, who are bilateral, i.e., sponsors donate funds to clubs, providing various services in their honor. The most important service includes the display of the sponsor's brand. Another exemplary service may include renting a skybox. The sponsorship ladder shows the most appreciation for the benefits of the strategic sponsor, who is given a central place on the players' jersey.

A large part of the clubs' budgets includes revenues from television broadcasts, which are distributed in different countries. Most often, they are affected by the rank in the table, but there is also a fixed part in this "equation". The remaining revenues may originate from football associations or tournament organizers, e.g., in connection with contracts with sponsors and bookmaker services, as well as various benefits from municipalities, for example in the form of a subsidy for renting a stadium, youth sports, or promoting the city. Other sources of income for clubs involve player transfers, commercial space rental, loyalty programs, and other.

In the early 1990s, football clubs entered the path of professionalization and commercialization (Rohde and Breuer, 2017; Totten, 2016). Since then, they have increased their revenues, but there are still certain difficulties as regards covering their costs. Some authors argue that clubs operate under the so-called soft budget constraint (Kornai, 1998; Storm and Nielsen, 2012). Football clubs are intensely focused on results and strive to achieve the set targets even at the expense of an unbalanced budget. At the same time, they gamble and assume that they will cover any debts from revenues related to future, but uncertain successes, or that they will be covered by the owner.

In an environment where gambling is present and there is focus on sports results, the increase in revenues of football clubs was mainly consumed by the salaries of players and, to a lesser extent, the commissions of football agents, e.g., PSG, Real Madrid, Manchester City. That said, these salaries have risen to astronomical amounts in mega-clubs. The most prominent football clubs even began to bypass the Financial Fair Play regulation, which assumed that clubs should not spend more than they earn.

The coronavirus pandemic and football games in the world

Like almost all organizations, football clubs are influenced by different trends in their surroundings. Some may threaten the continuity of their development by impacting the generated revenues. Such was the trend of the coronavirus pandemic. As a result, the beginning of 2020 transformed the conditions in which football clubs functioned. Individual leagues around the world began to suspend games. On January 30, the games were suspended in the Chinese Super League. It was clear that the virus was a global threat.

Along with its spread, authorities made similar decisions in other countries. In Kuwait, games stopped on February 24 and a few days later in Japan. The first non-Asian country to follow these footsteps was Switzerland (February 28). In subsequent days, leagues were suspended in Thailand (March 3), Iran (March 4), Italy (March 9), as well as Austria and Portugal (March 10). On March 11, the World Health Organization (WHO) announced the outbreak of the coronavirus pandemic, and recognized that the virus has likely spread to all countries of the world. Between March 12 and 14, football activities, including league games, were suspended in 41 countries. Between March 14 and March 18, a further 64 countries took the same measures. Thus, throughout seven days, 105 countries were suspended. On March 25, there were only three countries that played league games – Nicaragua, Burundi, and Belarus. The games in Tajikistan resumed on April 5. International games of national teams, such as the European, South American (Copa América), and Africa Championships, were moved to the next year (Tovar, 2021).

All these measures were necessary as mass events contributed to the spread of the coronavirus. An example of such an event was Cheltenham Festival in the UK, a horse racing event that took place from March 10 to 13, 2020, which attracted over 250,000 spectators in 4 days. Another event was the UEFA Champions League between Liverpool Football Club and Atletico Madrid at Liverpool's Anfield Stadium, which was held on March 11. There were 52,000 fans who attended the game, including 3,000 from Madrid. Spain was an early epicenter of the pandemic. There was also at least one Liverpool fan who went to the game feeling unwell, with symptoms of the coronavirus. Madrid's mayor later said the decision to allow the match had been a mistake. On April 24, the Liverpool mayor called for an independent investigation, which was undertaken by Liverpool City Council together with John Moores University and Liverpool University. However, a separate report was made by Edge Heath, which analyses health data for the National Health Service (NHS). Edge Heath performed modeling and estimated that the Liverpool vs. Atletico Madrid game was linked to additional deaths at local hospitals within Liverpool between days 25 and 35 after the game. The death toll associated with this match could, of course, have been higher, as it came from elsewhere in the UK, but also from Spain and other European countries. The analysis of the Edge Health data linked to the Cheltenham Festival showed 37 additional deaths in Gloucestershire hospitals alone (Moore, 2021).

The Champions League match in Italy was also considered a biological bomb. It was the 1/8 final match of the UEFA Champions League between Atalanta Bergamo and Spain's Valencia, which took place on February 19, 2020. Atalanta is based in Lombardy, which later became the epicenter of the coronavirus in Italy. According to UEFA rules, its stadium can only seat 21,000 people, so their home matches in the Champions League are played in Milan. Thirty miles away, at the San Siro Stadium, 40,000 fans came to the game against Bergamo and 4,000 from Valencia. According to the mayor of Bergamo: "About 40,000 Bergamo residents traveled to Milan to watch the game. Others watched it from their homes, in their families, in groups, at the bar. There was a situation this evening where the virus was widespread. Unfortunately, we couldn't know. Nobody knew the virus was already here. It was inevitable" (Moore, 2021).

Historical football events began to be mentioned in the media. Even after the games were resumed, whenever the fans returned to the stadiums, it was only for part of the matches and in a limited number. For example, the league in Germany was suspended on March 13, and the restart was scheduled for May 16 without spectators, therefore it was dubbed a "ghost game" (*Geisterspiele*) (Horky, 2021). However, this allowed for the preservation of revenues from broadcast rights, which constitute a significant part of budgets of up to 50% in clubs that play at the highest league levels of almost all countries (Tovar, 2021).

In these challenging times, players were expected to reduce their salaries, make donations or promote various social campaigns. The greatest international football stars, such as Lionel Messi or Cristiano Ronaldo, decided to cut their huge salaries. Messi and his teammates were now receiving less by 70%. They backed the decision to keep the salary at a 100% rate for other club employees. Ronaldo made a $1.8 million donation to fight COVID-19 to a hospital in Portugal (Kampmark, 2021).

Interestingly, measures to reduce salaries were not pursued in all leagues. In England, many clubs decided to take employees' leave and leave players' salaries at the same level, which was met with much political and public criticism. The clubs on vacation belonged to the wealthiest group, for example Liverpool, Tottenham, Newcastle, Norwich, or Bournemouth. According to the Global Sports Salary Survey, the average salary of a Premier League player in the 2018/2019 season was £3 million. Manchester clubs announced that they would pay total wages to players and other club employees (Kampmark, 2021).

On April 3, the Premier League hinted in a statement that it would ask players for a 30% cut or deferment of wages. This left unsatisfied footballers who had not been consulted beforehand. Most players were ready to cut their salaries, not as a favor to their clubs, but in order to donate this money to charities to support the National Health Service (NHS). As a result, over the next few days individual Premier League clubs and their players agreed to cut wages and defer their pay-outs. However, attacks on players fueled by the media and the public negatively impacted players' pay during the pandemic. A YouGov poll conducted on April 1 showed that 92% of the British believed that players should be prepared for a wage cut, and 67% of respondents believed that players should lower their wages by at least 50%. However, some pointed out that the public had not been surveyed on the remuneration of CEOs of major PLC companies, City of London bankers, or hedge fund managers (Moore, 2021).

The largely unfair and rather hostile image presented by the media of the response of Premier League players to the crisis was mainly been changed by the actions of one single player, Manchester United's Marcus Rashford. Rashford joined forces with the FareShare charity, an organization dealing with poverty and food waste. The initiative raised over £20 million to provide food for children who would receive free school meals if they were still in school during the closure. Rashford revealed that his family experienced food shortage when he was growing up. The project was initially developed to provide meals to children in the Greater Manchester area, but it was later expanded to become a national initiative involving over three million children nationwide. When the UK government tried to stop the extension of free school meals for children during the summer holidays, Rashford wrote an open letter on June 15. His actions were met with intense media and public support. A YouGov poll conducted on June 16 found that 63% of the respondents favored Rashford's viewpoint, and only 25% were against it. Rashford himself has done a lot to improve the damaged public image of the Premier League players as a whole. Since Rashford is black, his efforts seemed to resonate powerfully as Black Lives Matter became a global problem after George Floyd's death on May 25 (Moore, 2021).

The social activities were also joined by English clubs. For example, Chelsea FC delivered 115,000 meals through the Imperial College Healthcare NHS Trust to 5 local hospitals, made the Millennium and Copthorne Hotel on Stamford Bridge (the club's stadium) available to the National Health Service, and provided shelter, funding, and support to educate women and children experiencing domestic violence during the pandemic. By contrast, Manchester United FC and Manchester City FC organized a joint charity action #ACITYUNITED, and donated £100,000 for the purchase of bulk goods, which were later distributed by national food banks such as the Trussel Trust (Horky, 2021).

The social aspect was another element undertaken by football clubs during the COVID-19 pandemic. Exemplary activities undertaken by English Premier League clubs include:

- donating lunch box packages to organizations supporting the homeless;
- delivering educational packages for primary and secondary school students;
- contacting older people who are in isolation;
- cooperation with local authorities in the field of financing food banks and their distribution;
- re-purpose of hotel facilities belonging to clubs and their use for critical employees;
- delivering food parcels and offering mental support and advice in this regard;

- supporting vulnerable children and young people from the families of critical employees;
- handover of stadium facilities for the needs of health care;
- obtaining and transferring personal protective equipment for critical employees;
- donations to help victims of domestic violence and shelters;
- donating money, it equipment, cars, emergency materials for local education, health care, and social assistance;
- offering advice to applicants for benefits, medical examinations, stadium midwifery services, and mental health classes (Kennedy and Kennedy, 2021).

Never before has there been such a precedent before the games. Even during the Second World War, football was stopped only in some countries, such as Poland. However, it is worth mentioning that our country hosted occasional matches, such as the duel between Wisła Kraków and Garbarnia in 1942, which was watched by 1,500 fans. By contrast, World War II had little effect on football in South America. At that time, coaches and players were often fighting on the front lines. Nevertheless, things were different during the pandemic, and they can even be considered as its victims. Since the inception of international football, it has never been closed almost completely (Tovar, 2021).

Certainly, local epidemics occasionally disrupted football and other sports, such as the Ebola virus epidemic that spread in 2014 in several African countries. In 1972, the outbreak of the Yugoslav smallpox led to the cancellation of the national football league from March 26 to April 16. There are undoubtedly many other examples all over the world, but the scale was not like the coronavirus pandemic (Moore, 2021).

Football in England resumed on June 17, but the audience could watch it only on TV, and it returned merely in a minimal form with Premier League and the Championship. On April 3, the Premier League agreed to donate £125 million to the English Football League, but this was an advance on payments that had to be made later, not a donation. It was also not enough to solve the financial problems of lower league clubs caused by the pandemic. Mainly for economic reasons, the First and Second Leagues, all other men's leagues, and the Women's Super League voted to abandon the season. There is no doubt that the return of only two top men's leagues and the final FA Cup rounds did not serve primarily to uplift the nation, but the financial reality of TV rights deals. It is not clear why the Premier League did not purchase pandemic insurance. In 2003, the SARS outbreak taught the All England Lawn Tennis Club (AELTC) to purchase pandemic insurance for £1.5 million a year. By canceling the Wimbledon Championships in 2020, the AELTC will receive an estimated payout of approximately £114 million. Over 17 years, it has paid out about £25.5 million in premiums, which makes this insurance a wise investment (Moore, 2021).

The football world could not return to balance for a long time, and the threat of further pandemic waves only increased this uncertainty; it also disrupted the development of football clubs around the world. It was no different in Poland. The pandemic also had a considerable impact on domestic football clubs.

The coronavirus pandemic and the football games in Poland in the spring round of the 2020/2021 season

The first instances of COVID-19 were recorded in China in November and December of 2019. However, Poland took note of official cases at the beginning of March. Aware of the situation in the world, the regulators in Poland proceeded reasonably quickly. This was also true for professional football. On March 10, the authorities canceled mass open space events. According to the law, mass events in open areas gather at least 1,000 people. On March 12, 2020, the Management Board of the Polish Football Association (PZPN) met and, after consultations with football clubs, decided to continue the first and second league matches organized by the Association according to the schedule. However, the situation was dynamic, and there was growing public concern about the pandemic. On March 13, some of the professional football clubs announced that they would not be playing another match due to concerns for their health. For this reason, the Polish Football Association decided to cancel the 23rd round of the first and second league, of which it is the organizer. It also asked the company Ekstraklasa S.A., which manages the highest football league in Poland, to analyze the situation and make the appropriate decision.

On March 16, the Polish Football Association issued a message that due to the spreading coronavirus and the threat of pandemic, the next two rounds of the first and second league would be canceled, and that they would be played as soon as possible. The situation of the football clubs was becoming more and more precarious. On March 20, PZPN canceled all competitions until April 26.

In the following days, due to high uncertainty as to the development of the external situation, other decisions were made. It was not known whether the date of the European Championship matches would be changed or not. This also had an impact on the domestic games. Initially, due to this competition, UEFA recommended ending the domestic games. The representative of football clubs were concerned that this would affect their financial situation. If the league were canceled, sponsors would not pay or demand reimbursement of benefits due to the year in which the contracts were performed. Not all agreements include a provision for holding clubs responsible in the event of force majeure.

On April 1, 2020, a UEFA conference with the participation of national federations was held, and the topic of extending the 2019/2020 season and ending the games was raised. No specific arrangements were made at that time. There were two ending dates on June 30, when the contracts of some players usually end, and on July 20, which is the deadline for UEFA entries for the European cups. In the latter case, the 2020/2021 season would start in September 2020. If the games were not completed, the most likely scenario would be a promotion from the lower divisions, with no relegation, which would increase the volume of leagues and the number of matches. The decisions of the national unions were to be taken after those of the state authorities, so in May 2020 at the earliest.

Due to the potentially tricky situation of the clubs, the Polish Football Association offered them help. In March, it figured out how this help would proceed. In the 2020/2021 season, clubs from the Ekstraklasa, I, II, and III leagues received a total funding of PLN 50 million, and prizes for participation in each stage of the Polish Cup at the higher level increased by half.

In total, the entire package was estimated at over PLN 116 million. PZPN also decided that the players would now be able to apply for contract termination due to the club's fault only after a four, and not two-month, delay in payments. The clubs would be able to cut football players' salaries by half, which was also consented by Ekstraklasa S.A. This co-financing was as follows: for Ekstraklasa clubs – PLN 30 million, for the first league – PLN 10 million, second league – PLN 6 million, and third league – PLN 4 million. In addition, the Polish Football Association established that it would continue to run the Pro Junior System program at the current level. The total amount allocated to this purpose is PLN 18,100,000.

It was only in May that the pandemic situation in Poland improved and PZPN decided that football clubs would officially return to group training after examining the footballers and staff for the presence of coronavirus antibodies. The PZPN Medical Commission gave its consent each time. By May 13, all clubs from the 2nd league had been approved. The league authority resumed on June 3 and lasted until July 25. The situation required the extension of some contracts, which were usually set to end at the scheduled termination of the season on June 30. Initially, the matches were played without the participation of the public; this did not change until June 20, and only to a limited extent. Clubs could now fill only a quarter of the stadium. In the last round, the authorities changed this restriction, and it was possible to fill the stadium in half.

Widzew Łódź – characteristics of the club and the impact of the pandemic on its functioning

Characteristics of the club

Widzew Łódź is one of the most successful and famous football clubs in Poland. It was founded in 1910, but its most splendid successes can be dated back to the late seventies, eighties, and nineties, when it won the title of Polish Champion four times (1981, 1982, 1996, and 1997), seven times the title of the runner-up, and three times the lowest step of the podium. In 1985, the club won the Polish Cup. It was also a two-time winner of the Intertoto

Cup, a semi-finalist of the European Champions Clubs Cup, a participant in the group stage of the UEFA Champions League, the knockout stage of the UEFA Cup, and the Cup Winners' Cup. Widzew ranks 9th in the all-time table of the Polish Ekstraklasa. The club has been present in the top division for 35 seasons with 1,075 matches played, 425 wins, 1,401 goals scored, and 1,362 points won.

The club plays matches in Łódź in a relatively new stadium, which was built by the city and officially opened on March 18, 2017. The stadium has one-tier stands with a capacity of 18,018 seats in 4 stands; the entire audience is covered.

However, Widzew has not celebrated any triumphs in recent years. In 2015, the club collapsed and started anew in the 4th league (the 5th league level in Poland); it has now been systematically climbing to the top. In 2020, Widzew Łódź was promoted to the second level. The club has a lot of loyal fans who have been heavily involved in its reconstruction. Since the construction of the new stadium, they have been one of the largest audiences in Poland, with all available season tickets purchased. The club owns the Polish sales record, with 16,401 tickets sold in recent years.

Impact of the COVID-19 pandemic on the Widzew Łódź club: Organizational and financial analysis

The COVID-19 pandemic has had a considerable impact on the functioning of football clubs, including Widzew Łódź, this concern both the sports and organizational aspects.

The onset of the coronavirus came as a surprise. Nobody knew how long the pandemic would persist. In addition, more and more football clubs began to wonder how the pandemic would affect their financial situation, and it was no different in Widzew. Behind the scenes, discussions had been taking place already from the beginning of the pandemic. The decisions of the Polish Football Association were followed on an ongoing basis.

At the beginning of April, the supervisory board convened a meeting. The management board, together with the members of the management board of the RTS Widzew Łódź Association were invited. The Widzew's

Management Board was asked to prepare financial projections considering various scenarios related to the continuation or suspension of the games.

Discussions were started concerning the financial situation of the club and the impact of the coronavirus pandemic on revenues and costs. Widzew's authorities draw attention to problems with benefits for sponsors, as well as the possible threats. In the event of non-resumption of the games or resumption of the competition without the fans, changes to the contract and reduction of payments would be made. The management of the club started contacting and negotiating new conditions with the sponsors. Ultimately, the sponsors proved that some benefits hadn't been met despite the club's efforts, and reduced payments to PLN 600,000.

Another source of income at risk was income from lodge tenants. The lodges were rented as stadium offices with access seven days a week to the tenants. This provided partial protection to the club from possible claims. On the other hand, most lodges were used only on match day. The club was also not interested in coming into conflict with the lodge tenants. Pursuant to this fact, the club employee responsible for business contacts would contact the tenants. Later, when it was possible, he would also hand over occasional gifts. During the pandemic, two lodge tenants decided to resign. It was not a severe problem for the club, as their place was quite easily obtained by two more companies that had already tried to rent the boxes and had been on the waiting list.

Widzew has a revenue structure that is specific for Polish conditions, namely a large part of it comes from the sale of passes. There was a concern that people who bought season tickets could apply for a refund due to the inability to watch the matches. Because the fans were heavily involved in the club's reconstruction, they understood that this could worsen its situation. There were only a few cases of refund. However, the pandemic did not remain without any impact on the revenues from ticket sales. Since the club's stands are filled by the holders of season ticket, Widzew introduced a seat release system when a season ticket holder would be unable to attend a match. Based on previous seasons, the club's budget assumed that, on average, three thousand people would vacate the seats during every game. The club could not realize this revenue due to the pandemic.

In addition to reducing revenues, Widzew's authorities also addressed cost reduction. The personnel costs in sports clubs are an essential element. After joint arrangements with the club's authorities, the management began negotiating the reduction of players' salaries in the following months. If the players did not agree to the reductions, the only way to make this possible would be through court proceedings. Withholding the salaries of football players is a serious problem with environmental laws protecting wages. Under normal circumstances, if the club does not pay for three months, the player may terminate the contract due to the club's fault. However, this does not release it from settlement of the entire amount resulting from the agreement. During the pandemic, the Polish Football Association extended this period to four months. If payments to foreign players are suspended, they may submit disputes directly to the International Court of Arbitration for Sport in Lausanne (CAS), which hears the cases under Swiss law.

Ultimately, the negotiations with the players, which the management board undertook after consultation with the supervisory board, were successful. For four months between April and July, the wages of players were cut by 40%, and for those less paid – by 30%. President Martyna Pajączek said, "There was no fair, there was no indifference, and putting aside a complicated topic. Together, we concluded that in this challenging time, it is necessary to act in solidarity. We quickly agreed on the terms, but the formalities were more time-consuming. We cannot allow Widzew's future to be in danger, so the funds we have must last a little longer than until June, so we have to save". The reductions also included members of the management board, employees of the club, and the Widzew Football Academy.

Additionally, Widzew Łódź applied to the Polish Development Fund for public aid offered to entrepreneurs to counter the effects of COVID-19. The application was accepted, and the club received funds related to the so-called first anti-crisis shield of PLN 934,328.00; this figure was to be largely written off. It has been estimated that the club will have to repay 25% of this amount in 24 monthly interest-free installments, starting from the 13th month from the date of payment of the subsidy.

Despite reducing costs during the pandemic, it still influenced the revenues and the financial result. After the budget update, it turned out that the club's revenues had fallen by PLN 2,152 thousand, but costs by only about 1,093 thousand. Hence, the financial result of Widzew in 2020 was negative.

Impact of the COVID-19 pandemic on the Widzew Łódź club: Analysis of the sports aspect

In the 2019/2020 season, Widzew Łódź, which had rebuilt itself after bankruptcy, was fighting for promotion to the 2nd league, i.e., to the first league in Poland. After an unsuccessful 2018/2019 season, when the club lost its chance for a promotion in the last matches, the management and approach to team building changed. One of the reasons for failure was intense pressure from the fans, which the players could not cope with. The new management transformed the team, basing it on experienced players, often with a history of playing in the league, who had their best years behind them. One example is Marcin Robak who was brought in to the club. Robak was already 36 years old at the time, but he was a nine-time representative of Poland. In the previous season, he had become the top scorer in Ekstraklasa in the colors of Śląsk Wrocław. The new players also had high contracts that would be extended if promoted to a higher league, which served to motivate them to achieve their goals. According to union regulations, they would simultaneously be increased by twenty percent after the promotion. Contracts also included individual bonuses, and the team would receive a specific team bonus.

The 2019/2020 season did not start well. In the first six matches, it scored only 8 points, including two lost games. However, after the initial loss of the new team, it quickly started to climb, and at the end of 2019, it ranked first in the table. In the first two matches in the new year, the team scored 4 points, including a victory in the away game against the runner-up Górnik Łęczna. It seemed that the club would get into shape and consistently pursue the promotion to a higher league. However, two days before the next match, the games were suspended due to the coronavirus.

During the pandemic outbreak, the players were forced to stop training and go home. Some clubs in Poland broke this ban. For example, the players of Arka Gdynia were caught during training. Meanwhile, the players and coaches at Widzew went home and were supposed to train remotely, which was to be supervised by the training staff and the management. Of course, this was pretty tricky during the lockout, and there were assumptions that the players wouldn't be training conscientiously. Indeed, individual training alone could not be effective in team sports.

The players in Widzew returned to group training on May 10, 2020, and the games were resumed after an almost three-month break on June 3. Widzew played the last match before the break on March 8. Thus, the players remained without training for two and a half months. In a team with a high average age, this would have a more significant impact on the players' sports condition. The break paired with the salary cuts gave rise to conflicts between the players, for example between some players and the team captain, which broke the team spirit.

All these problems influenced athletic performance. After the resumption of the games, Widzew Lodz played 12 matches, of which it only won 3 and another 3 were tied. The club lost in 6 games, including the last 2 rounds. As for in-home matches, Widzew recorded 4 defeats and 2 victories. In the previous round, it lost to Znicz Pruszków. It seemed that the almost certain promotion to the first league now depended on the matches of other teams.

Eventually, Widzew Łódź advanced to the 1st league thanks to a draw of the main rival GKS Katowice in the last round and a better balance of goals with an equal number of points. It is worth mentioning that in the last minutes of the match, the players of GKS Katowice hit the goalpost. The promotion satisfied neither the management nor the fans. After the last whistle of the referee, some of them actually stepped into the pitch, and there was a struggle with the players. Despite the promotion, the coach was also dismissed after the season. The atmosphere around the club was terrible.

The impact of the pandemic on the club's CSR activities. Despite progressive professionalization, football clubs still have strong ties with their communities. The aim is to be treated not as business entities but rather organizations that combine economic and social activity. Club communities (fans) identify strongly with the clubs and feel like a part of them. Football clubs and their fans make every effort to support one another, in particular in the area of CSR. Hence, CSR strategies have become an essential part of club strategies and building their identity and image (Breitbarth and Harris, 2008; Fifka and Jaeger, 2020).

During the pandemic, the significance of conventional club management decreased. Instead, they undertook more CSR activities, often directing them towards groups that needed help during this period. However, the initiative of Widzew Łódź belonged to the fan community, and the club merely supported it. On March 19, one of the two fanatics associations launched an online initiative "Widzew for Hospitals". The original target was to collect PLN 19,100 for personal protection and food for hospitals. Surprisingly, supporters of the initiative managed to achieve this within twenty-four hours. Therefore, they decided that they would continue the collection.

The second goal was to raise PLN 110,000. This particular amount was chosen due to the 110th anniversary of Widzew Łódź which took place in 2020. The fans encouraged one another through nominations on social media. Many even donated PLN 19.10, referring to the year in which the club was founded; there were also others who paid higher amounts. Furthermore, the club was involved in a fundraising campaign, which it promoted on its websites and social media. Representatives made payments to the owner (Stowarzyszenie RTS Widzew Łódź), the supervisory board, the management board, club employees, as well as current and former footballers. Over 2,000 people took part in the action. The second goal was already achieved on March 26. The president of Widzew Martyna Pajączek, who also personally supported the #WidzewDlaSzpitali, said "You can always count on our fans. I am proud that they organized this fundraiser. I would like to thank the entire Widzew community for their significant commitment to achieving such an important and beautiful goal. It is difficult to say when we will defeat the coronavirus, but I am sure that we will do it thanks to such actions."

After the supporters collected the target amount, the collection continued and quickly reached PLN 157,220. In total, 2,437 people made payments. Additionally, the fundraising initiative received gifts from some companies, for example, one of the producers donated nine pallets of items such as paper towels and handkerchiefs.

The collected funds and gifts were distributed among various health care institutions. Initially, the initiators of collections selected 14 institutions. Later, they expanded that list to include medical facilities not only from Łódź and the surrounding area but also from other parts of the country, i.e., in the Mazowieckie, Greater Poland, and Świętokrzyskie Voivodeships. The action was a media success, and it was widely commented on various portals. It certainly had a positive impact on the image of the club and the fans at that time. Some local Widzew fan clubs carried out similar actions and transferred the collected funds to local institutions.

Conclusion

The article describes the management-related problems faced by football clubs in connection with the coronavirus pandemic in early 2020. As an example, the authors described the Polish professional club Widzew Łódź, which played on the third level. Despite this fact, it is a very popular club in Poland. The low level of the game was related to the club's recovery after bankruptcy. Consequently, most of the described problems also apply to clubs playing at a higher level.

The coronavirus pandemic has caused many problems in both the organizational and sporting spheres of football clubs, with which the authorities of these organizations had to cope. These tasks were challenging. The described case clearly demonstrates the significance of the environment in strategy and current operation of enterprises. The coronavirus pandemic has led to severe problems in many industries. It hindered the implementation of plans, caused tensions on the part of stakeholders, and led to changes in management boards. The depth of the turbulence surprised many owners and managers.

However, the article concerns primarily football clubs, which are specific organizations that remain in a strong symbiosis with their fans. At the same time, financial results are not their most important aspect, since sports results take precedence over them. Indeed, the financial element is expected by the communities, sponsors, local authorities, and other stakeholders. Such pressure can be disruptive and lead to financial problems, which has been the case in many clubs worldwide due to the pandemic. The most famous examples include Spanish clubs, especially FC Barcelona, whose financial failure has been exposed by the pandemic.

Clubs cannot equate their fans with clients of other companies since their bond with clubs is much stronger. Fawbert (Fawbert 2017) said that nobody spreads their grandfather's ashes down the central aisle of Tesco's (supermarket), but every day of the week, somebody is spreading someone's ashes on a football pitch in England. It is more like a disciple going to a temple. All actions taken by fans are carried out under the club's brand name, which can be disadvantageous considering hooliganism or violence. Still, on the other hand, fans can positively impact the club's brand by building social campaigns. One such example is the action undertaken by Widzew fans "aid for hospitals", a grassroots initiative that was widely echoed throughout the country.

This article refers to the specific situation related to the impact of COVID-19. Still, it may also serve as an inspiration for further analyses of a relatively new area of interest, which is the management of football clubs – something that evokes a lot of emotions, just like the game itself. In Poland, relatively few studies have been published on this subject. The available research is related mainly to marketing, international management, or the financial results and effectiveness of clubs; therefore, there are many gaps in this subject, which include, for example, the problems of strategic management in football clubs or the value management within them.

References

Breitbarth T. and Harris P. (2008). "The role of corporate social responsibility in the football business: Towards the development of a conceptual model". *European Sport Management Quarterly* 8(2), 179–206.

Fawbert J. (2017). West Ham United in the Olympic Stadium: A Gramscian analysis of the rocky road to Stratford. In: *London 2012 and the Post-Olympics City: A Hollow Legacy*, P. Cohen and P. Watt (eds.) (259–286). London: Palgrave Macmillan.

Fifka M. and Jaeger J. (2020). "CSR in professional European football: An integrative framework". *Soccer and Society* 21(1), 61–78.

Horky T. (2021). "No sports, no spectators – no media, no money? The importance of spectators and broadcasting for professional sports during COVID-19". *Soccer and Society* 22(1–2), 96–102.

Kampmark B. (2021). "Are we all in this together? Footballing ethics in the age of Coronavirus". *Soccer and Society* 22(1–2), 115–124.

Kennedy D. and Kennedy P. (2021). "English Premier League football clubs during the COVID-19 pandemic: Business as usual?". *Soccer and Society* 22(1–2), 27–34.

Kornai J. (1998). "The place of the soft budget constraint syndrome in economic theory". *Journal of Comparative Economics* 45, 1573–1599.

Kuper S. and Szymański S. (2019). *Futbonomia*. Kraków: Wydawnictwo SQN.

Moore K. (2021). "Football is not 'a matter of life and death'. It is far less important than that: Football and the COVID-19 pandemic in England". *Soccer and Society* 22(1–2), 43–47.

Polsat Sport (2020, April 24). *Widzew obniżył pensje piłkarzom i trenerom.* https://www.polsatsport.pl/wiadomosc/2020-04-24/widzew-obnizyl-pensje-pilkarzom-i-trenerom. Accessed: 20.05.2023.

Rohde M. and Breuer C. (2017). "The market for football club investors: A review of theory and empirical evidence from professional European football". *European Sport Management Quarterly* 17(3), 265–289.

Sport TVP (2020, March 26). *Piękny gest kibiców Widzewa. Dynamiczna zbiórka pieniędzy dla szpitala.* https://sport.tvp.pl. Accessed: 20.05.2023.

Storm R. and Nielsen K. (2012). "Soft budget constraints in professional football". *European Sport Management Quarterly* 12(2), 183–201.

Totten M. (2016). "Football and community empowerment: How FC Sankt Pauli fans organize to influence". *Soccer and Society* 17(5), 703–720.

Tovar J. (2021). "Soccer, World War II and coronavirus: A comparative analysis of how the sport shut down". *Soccer and Society* 22(1–2), 66–74.

Marta Brzozowska, Ph.D.
Jan Kochanowski University of Kielce

Dorota Dziedzic, Ph.D.
Krakow University of Economics

Katarzyna Kolasińska-Morawska, Ph.D.
Krakow University of Economics

Resilient parts of logistic chains as a way to survive the COVID-19 pandemic

Abstract

Today, the global syntactic world marked by digitization, biotechnology and permeates almost every area of socio--economic functioning of individuals and organizations. On the one hand, accelerating the "heartbeat" of multiplicative change, the wealth of information as well as the knowledge of generations stimulates development, and heralds the arrival of Society 5.0 and Economy 5.0. But on the other hand, wars together with climatic and biological disasters cause economic slowdown up to the state of emergence. The black swan pandemic, or SARS-CoV-2, will trigger a wave of change. Global delivery systems implemented by interconnected entities have been put to the test. The stoppage of production in factories, the suspension of transports and the inability to move people due to international lockdown have forced the managers of global supply chains to redefine their methods of operation. The key to surviving these difficult days is resilience, which together with flexibility and sensitivity, by its nature, is able to cope with changes, especially those with quantification of risk occurring in a discontinuous environment. The aim of the article is to discuss ways to maintain competitive advantage based on the concept of resilient supply chain in the face of the omnipresent threat that is the SARS-CoV-2 pandemic. Data for this purpose was obtained from both secondary and primary sources by means of a mixed qualitative and quantitative methodology. The literature allowed for employment of monographic methods, specifically content analysis. The comparative case study technique was applied to obtain the primary material. We used the collected material to prepare the guidelines for adapting the methods of supply chain management to new challenges — not only in the post-pandemic reality, but above all in the uncertain future, in which enterprises operating within the structures of supply chains may face more than one "swan" threat.

Keywords: resilient supply chains, SARS-CoV-2 pandemic, flexibility and adaptation, digitization and automation, competitive advantage

Introduction

The future of logistics and supply chains is built primarily upon the foundation of IT tools. The fourth industrial revolution, which the literature refers to as Industry 4.0[1], indicates new directions for the development of not only logistics but the entire industry. Innovativeness in the entire logistics industry was put to the test during the pandemic. Technological investments have proven crucial, however, it was clear that organizational relations, which comprise the base of logistics functioning, were a vital element for business continuity. Interestingly, logistics itself as well as its basic processes secured the existence of not only enterprises, but entire societies. This was possible firstly by taking care of the supply of the necessary protective measures, medicines or even something as simple as food. When the whole world stopped, logistics, i.e., transport, warehouses, production were the only elements of the economy that could provide basic food, hygiene and health products. This was evident in everyday news broadcast around the world.

The coronavirus crisis has shocked the European, and even the global economy. But it did not stop there, as it also disturbed the continuity of economic activities due to various restrictions and legal conditions. For example, ensuring a smooth supply of raw materials, products or the provision of services has become a challenge (Poudel et al., 2020). Globalization, which has been considered one of the basic conditions for economic development to date, has also contributed to the spread of the SARS-CoV-2 virus. With the movement of people and products, the virus "travelled" from Asia to the rest of the world. Thus, in order to stop the virus, it was necessary to stop global traffic. This gave rise to a number of economic problems. The impact of the pandemic on mobility was noticeable, but at the same time the availability of the products to the public had to be ensured (Allam, 2020).

The fact that global movement has been restricted or that travel has been completely suspended in some countries is not enough. The pandemic caused

---

[1] Currently, we are talking about the next industrial revolution, i.e., the fifth generation, which results from technological development and focuses primarily on the cooperation of man and machine.

many cascading effects for the economy, which are just beginning to emerge only now after a dozen months. Particularly strongly felt is the decline of economic activity in China and the closely related Asian economies, as well as the disruptions of global value chains, which is partaken by companies from the EU and the US that import components from these locations. To prevent the spread of the epidemic in China, the authorities have introduced a number of restrictions, including factory closures and quarantine for workers. This resulted in a strong decline in industrial and service-related activity. The effects of the reduction in demand were felt in many countries and by various industries, including transport (especially air transport), gastronomy, tourism and entertainment.

The core effect was the economic crisis, caused mainly by the delayed implications of the restrictions in the form of suspended production and supplies, the closure of enterprises, and the inability to provide services. The first economic forecasts focused primarily on highly developed countries and indicated that these economies would lose a few percent of their GDP (Chetan and Yogish, 2020). Disruptions in value chains have resulted in a decline in production, competitiveness, and market share. Resilience of the supply chain is often highly desirable, as it increases corporate readiness in dealing with possible risks from the customers' side, the suppliers' side, as well as the adopted internal processes and the employed supply chain integration mechanisms. However, though the practitioners responsible for the design and management of supply networks often perceive resilience as highly desirable, they also take note of the direct costs of this trade-off (Purvis et al., 2016).

The global economy is just beginning to recover from the crisis in 2020. The GDP in individual countries is on the rise, for example the USA is seeing noticeable growth but not as large as expected (bankier.pl, 2021). The GDP in the euro area is also growing with a simultaneous low inflation (ec.europa.eu, 2021). The economy of the eurozone will continue to rise by 3.8% in both 2021 and 2022. The forecast also predicts that the EU economy will grow by 3.7% in 2021 and 3.9% in 2022 (ec.europa. eu, 2021). The Polish economy is also performing quite well against this background, since the GDP here is also growing as well. What is more, the Polish economy is expected to be one of the fastest recovering, with the estimated GDP growth exceeding 5 percentage points. However, the situation induced by inflation, which, according to data from the second quarter, amounted to slightly over 5%, is in fact worrying (bankier.pl, 2021). But similar problems are also observed in the US economy.

In view of such predictions, it is certainly important to rebuild economic relations after the pandemic downtime. This will definitely be a challenge in the coming years. The year 2021 showed how much the economies of individual countries are interdependent and to what extent globalization affects the economy. Problems carried over from pandemic downtime are now noticeable in production in factories of European cars or electronic products. Mainly there is a shortage of semiconductors that support on-board computers or electronic devices such as computers, laptops and smartphones (Poitiers and Weil, 2021; Xiling, 2021). Due to the deficit of micro-chips, car assembly lines in Europe have come to a halt. This is one example of how global supply chains operate. The decline in the production of car equipment in Chinese factories amounted to −28.2%; this is a decrease of 13.5% for the entire production (Coveri et al., 2020). The forecasts, especially those for the automotive industry, were rather poor. We can say with confidence that if it had not been for the restrictive approach to restrictions, the crisis would have been even more tangible (Guan et al., 2020).

The changes induced by the pandemic will surely be felt in the global economy for a long time. Hence, it is important to adapt to these changes, as well as to other economic conditions. Supply chains also need to transform their nature, mainly in terms of organization. In recent years, most logistics and production companies have invested heavily in technologically advanced solutions supporting communication processes, but on the other hand, the need to maintain appropriate relationships between individual links in the supply chain has been forgotten. Jointly building value for the client as well as for the chain participants seems essential at this point.

This article highlights crucial changes in the organization of supply chains that will help them resist unforeseen events and maintain a competitive advantage. The aim of the article is to discuss ways to maintain competitive advantage based on the concept of resilient supply chain in the face of the omnipresent threat that is the SARS-CoV-2 pandemic.

Complexity and transformations of supply chains in the view of current megatrends

Today, most organizations act as merely components of complex structures. Logistic processes focused around the internal sphere of enterprises are increasingly becoming a component of larger, more complex and multidimensional systems, i.e., supply chains. Such complexity was also reflected in the attempt to quantify the terminology, or rather its unified formula (Harland et al., 2006). In terms of operationalization, the supply chain, ambiguous in its assignment to scientific disciplines, demonstrates its dual essence in reference to theory and practice, conciliatingly combining a scientific approach with a business application. The significant impact of transformations that take place in the environment, including globalization, digitization and technologization, resulting in the growing importance of networking, is exemplified in the definition of the supply chain.

In terms of the network, the supply chain can be defined as "a network of producers and service providers who cooperate with each other to process and move goods - from the raw material phase to the level of end users" (Bozarth and Handfield, 2021), or "a network of partners who as part of a joint operation, they transform the basic raw material (supply phase) into a finished product (distribution phase) with a specific value for end buyers and manage returns at each stage" (Harrison and Hoek, 2010, p. 34). The structure and functioning of supply chains is integrally intertwined with the environment. Supply chains, being firmly embedded in the environment, remain in constant interaction with it. The evolving environment contributes to changes in supply chains. Geopolitics, innovation, robotization and automation, technologies such as IoT, AI, big data, blockchain, the doctrine of sustainable development versus labor deficit, climate crises, "post-Brexit", financial crises caused by speculative and biological bubbles will contribute to redefining activities and processes.

The nature and strength of the impact of changes varies in time and space, and this in turn makes the adaptation processes of enterprises generally complex and multi-faceted (Zygmunt and Zygmunt, 2016). Especially times of crises (Gryz and Kitler, 2007; Nepelski, 2016; Michałowska et al., 2015), which persist for a certain time and contribute to transformation in the structures and operation of individual organizations and their networks, are associated with a state of increasing destabilization, uncertainty and tension, characterized by immersion of connections, the possibility of losing control and escalating threats. The SARS-CoV-2 virus pandemic is undoubtedly a representation of such a state. Finding solutions and introducing cushioning and remedial actions requires recognizing that the concept of applicability of regulations that exists in the risk management model is highly significant. Building procedures for dealing with the definition of roles, tasks and competences along with the identification of the causes of the crisis and potential consequences, combined with a quick response, can serve as a major remedy. Therefore, risk management solutions can enrich the form of supply chain operation with the desired capabilities that combine methods for reducing risk states, limiting the possibility of their occurrence and dealing with their adverse effects.

An effective management system should therefore be anti-crisis (Saleh, 2016), built taking into account the possibility of a crisis, and the inability to avoid it or delay it (Walas-Trębacz and Ziarko, 2010). The management of a crisis situation must be subject to general management principles, such as: setting goals, diagnosing the situation, selecting implementation measures and responsible persons, and controlling the effects (Zakrzewska-Bielawska, 2008). The quality of crisis management is vital for supply chains, and therefore the experience gained as a result of states and crisis situations is conducive to a breakthrough that can potentially enrich and streamline processes as well as procedures. After all, crises are becoming more frequent. At this point, the question of "Is the enterprise/supply chain in crisis?" loses significance. Especially in view of the experiences resulting from the SARS-CoV-2 pandemic, one should rather ask "When will a crisis occur?" and, regardless of temporal predictions, prepare for such an eventuality.

In this paper, we discuss resilient supply chains. Resilience is an emanation of complexity and dynamics that keeps the supply chain operational in uncertain times. In other words, a resilient supply chain has the ability to adapt, react reactive and regain lost forces. Therefore, it is fit with a mechanism by which it effectively faces changes that are uncertain and difficult to predict, i.e., those whose generator is primarily the environment of the supply chain's functioning. As supply chains become more complex as a result of global sourcing and the continued trend of "leaning-down", the risk associated with them increases. The challenge that business faces today is to manage and mitigate that risk through establishing more resilient supply chains (Christopher and Peck, 2004). Moreover, this capability allows firms to build the resiliency to mitigate enterprise risks (Lee and Rha, 2016).

There is a visible departure from linear supply chains in which events and operations are of a silo nature. In the face of the challenges in the digital economy, effective supply chains operating in network connectivity ecosystems have a reason to exist. The essence of this phenomenon is a synergistic cooperation based on the control tower concept co-created by employees from various departments. Experts make joint decisions not only for the organization as such, but also for cooperating entities, because coherence on the scale of the entire enterprise determines the possibility of achieving and maintaining a competitive advantage not only of a single entity, but also the entire supply chain. Nowadays, competition refers to supply chains. From that perspective, supply chain faces two major risks: disruption of suppliers and tough competition (Rezapour et al., 2017). Access to up-to-date data by means of digitization supports the feasibility of this concept. The effect is transparency and optimality, as well as duration and development, which makes it independent from the environment. In addition, the implementation of IT in collaboration with certain strategies allows to develop a resilient supply chain. Moreover, in case any of these risks occur, the possibility that an organization will bounce back and start operations in the shortest possible time is also considered (Mensah et al., 2015).

H.L. Lee described the threat to the security of supply chains in the context of uncertainties regarding lead times, customs procedures and transit, in the face of limited transparency (visibility) of transport processes (2004). The crisis forces a change in the state of behavior. Information sharing represents an important weapon for ensuring process safety and continuity (Log4.pl, 2020). Up-to-date and valuable information help to understand and react quickly to changes. Dynamic supply chains are evolving towards more open, optimal, and efficient structures. Interactivity and interoperability allow for faster, more efficient and more precise operation. Information technologies within economy 4.0 are conducive to increasingly accurate forecasting, which will allow more precise response to changing market conditions in the future.

Adaptive stabilization of resilient supply chains to the challenges of COVID-19

By definition, resilient supply chains are complex and open adaptive systems that operate in an uncertain environment. Here, uncertainty of environment means that it is impossible to predict (as is risk management) neither the source of origin, nor the probability of a risk factor (s), as well as the strength and direction of its negative or positive effects. Thus, the notion of responsive chain is based on the ex post concept, that is, a reaction to the consequences caused by factors of uncertainty that have already occurred. These factors are usually negative. Systems and the reactions that take place within them tend to stabilize. Balance in which a supply chain should remain comprises a system of relations between the environment and the organizations participating in this chain. It is worth noting that balance also applies to the interior of these organizations, and is measured by means of technical and operational indicators, financial indicators as well as an assessment of the degree of compliance between employee expectations regarding working and pay conditions and their actual fulfillment.

By adapting the relationship to changed conditions, the resilient supply chain can meet the expectations of both the environment and the participants of the organization. Maintaining the balance of the supply chain becomes the basis for achieving its goals. Unfortunately, the degree and extent of adjustments needed to maintain balance in the resilient supply chain is unpredictable. In the long term, these changes may lead to a redefinition of the current pattern of supply chain functioning and, as a consequence, temporarily or permanently change its elements and processes. This was also the case with the changes brought by the COVID-19 pandemic. The uncertainty concerning the consequences of falling ill and dying felt by hundreds of thousands around the world has disrupted the movement of people and goods. The situation was new – never before has a pandemic spread across the globe, and secondly, has the economies of countries been so heavily dependent on global supply chains. The lockdown of cities and borders suddenly broke supply chains. Production stopped in many locations around the world due to a shortage of raw materials and components.

In a short time, production priorities and delivery methods had to be redefined. Moreover, with the development of the pandemic, consumer behavior, as well as the demand for certain goods, changed. Optimal allocation of demand across a set of suppliers in a supply chain that is exposed to supply and environmental risk had to be considered. National movement restrictions, limitation or suspension of stationary sales, restaurant closures, and fear of contagion have all increased interest in mail order sales and purchase of food through applications or via the Internet. The stationary world made a leap towards the virtual world. The pandemic forced the acceleration of the digitization of information flows in supply chains and allowed to introduce countless innovations, thereby streamlining communication between individual participants.

The main adaptation activities of selected links in the supply chains to the COVID-19 challenges are presented below.

Operation of transport companies from the raw materials and goods market

The delivery of goods for production and trade at the right place and at the right time is the basis of a well-functioning economy. The COVID-19 pandemic, as well as increased health protection, and with it changing transport regulations, numerous illnesses in individual countries, unpredictability and uncertainty about the future, have all disrupted the current flow of goods. The economic effects of this situation in particular sectors and enterprises varied and were dependent on many factors, including corporate ability or propensity to build up inventories before the pandemic, distance from sources of supply, degree of dependence of production on external suppliers, or the ability to quickly find alternative sources of supply. Supply chains, on the one hand, were forced to become more flexible and react dynamically to further restrictions and changes to the "rules of the game", and on the other hand, to grapple with the uncertain shifts in consumer behavior, and thus to transformations in demand for individual goods and services. Both transport and production companies undertook joint activities aimed at developing a strategy that would ensure that, despite the pandemic, the operation of industry and trade remained uninterrupted. Strong relationships with key partners (recipients or suppliers) as well as the rapid flow of information between participants in the supply chain were of particular importance. The current, i.e., pre-pandemic, free movement of goods in EU countries collided with the closing of borders, restoration of border controls, sickness spreading among drivers and the reorganization of their work. These factors influenced the operation of production companies waiting for deliveries, as well as some stores. Transport enterprises, especially international ones, were operating under a strong pressure to quickly deliver both production and commercial goods. The decisions made by the European Commission regarding the creation of the so-called "Green lanes" reserved for lorries greatly facilitated transport, among others by minimizing procedures at border crossing points, as well as checks and inspections, eliminating the need for drivers to leave the cab. The delivery of goods was not only hindered by land, but also by sea, since the ports introduced restrictions for unloading. For example, Maersk canceled over 50 courses from China in two weeks of March 2020 (Smoleń, 2021). Also, air transport was completely abandoned for some time. The new business conditions for enterprises active in the supply chain have contributed to deepened digitization. Electronic document databases and digital pens were introduced on an increasing scale and their use greatly facilitated the circulation of CMR documents and enabled immediate data update by mobiles applications. It was also easier to conclude contracts and sign handover protocols remotely (IC Solutions Sp. z o.o., 2021). Thanks to electronic solutions, some operational areas of transport companies could be performed from home. In addition, a number of activities related to suppliers' monitoring was undertaken. Artificial intelligence proved helpful in this respect. One example is General Motors, which uses artificial intelligence to map delivery in order to accurately document the introduction of goods to the market. Another AI-powered solution is a platform used at a logistics company CH Robinson which enables end-to-end, flexible delivery management for dealing with potential disruptions. It constantly analyzes changes in the market which affect the throughput of commercial lanes in the air and in the oceans. The pandemic has seen the emergence of many similar solutions, which will be successively implemented in all distribution channels, making processes more flexible and optimizing post-pandemic supply chains.

Courier services market

During the pandemic, the courier market has in many cases replaced free movement. The inability to make stationary purchases meant that, along with the development of the pandemic and prolonged quarantine periods, the number of online purchases and smartphones increased. The link between e-commerce and the customer base are usually courier companies, which deliver products ordered online to customers who cannot collect them in person in a store or restaurant. This pandemic raised the interest in courier services and caused a rapid growth in demand for such services, especially since carriers did not stop operating both locally and globally. For customers ordering products by means of electronic tools, the key issues were: delivery time, variety of available products, payment method, reliability of delivery, friendly handling of returns and, above all, safety. Companies operating in the area of e-commerce supply chains therefore had to quickly adapt and improve their tools for communicating with potential customers. An easy-to-use application for ordering, tracking and collecting shipments (e.g., in parcel lockers), as well as a friendly website for both online stores and courier companies have become an indispensable competitive tool and often constituted one of the main factors in choosing a given method of delivery by Internet users. In response to market needs, DHL and UPS released shipment recipients from signing the courier scanner. DHL launched the "DHL for You" application, which allows to send parcels via phone, computer or tablet in less than 3 minutes, without leaving one's home. Before COVID-19, this was only possible for domestic shipments, but during the pandemic this service was also extended to international shipments (Tenerowicz, 2021). Contactless deliveries were becoming more and more common – parcels were left at the recipient's door. This option was usually used by courier companies delivering food products or meals from restaurants (Glovo, UberEats, BoltFood). In order to encourage customers to use parcel machines more often, InPost introduced a new service – Parcel on Weekend, which enabled deliveries to parcel machines also on Saturdays and Sundays. This was also a response to a survey conducted by InPost, in which 82% of the surveyed e-commerce representatives expressed their willingness to introduce the option of weekend delivery to parcel machines in their stores, 66% of the surveyed buyers described their recent purchases as urgent or very urgent, and 60% of customers of stores that had recently used courier delivery expressed their willingness to use this option (InPost, n.d.). Limiting the contact between the courier and the sender or recipient was not the only pandemic-related measure taken by courier companies to increase the safety of both employees and customers. Aware of the resulting threats, courier companies introduced numerous safeguards against the possible spread of the virus. New hygiene rules were introduced, e.g., creating new procedures (regarding employee behavior during receipt and issue of parcels), working with gloves and masks, frequent washing and disinfecting of hands, equipping departments with special preparations for disinfecting parcels.

Conclusion

To conclude, the issues that arose from the SARS-CoV-2 crisis resulted in the suspension of investments, delays in deliveries, shortages of products and components, and financial losses. Supply chains were under high pressure – the fluctuations in demand strained many of them, causing turmoil that will be felt for quite a long time. However, admittedly, the managers of pandemic supply chains have also gained experience that will support their decision-making processes in building resilient structures. Legal safeguards and more dynamic financial control should be the basis. The future belongs to functionally and infrastructural, modernized supply chains that are digitized.

Managers should ensure that there are real relationships in their chains that rely on open information exchange based on the cloud, as well as increase the emphasis placed on greater automation of transactions and virtualization of cooperation, including with carriers. Such an ecosystem approach will allow for architectural management that is founded on proactivity in shaping value within a turbulently changing environment. There are many ways to compete, which is mentioned in numerous studies. The state of emergency acts as a law of "surprise" that binds all interested parties with strong ties. Crises cannot be eliminated, completely, but it is possible to learn to live with it. Balancing between stability and destabilization strengthens and immunizes for the future. The essence is the ability to function resiliently while remaining flexible and adaptable, and bouncing back from adversity to return to the original state. Nevertheless, plasticity alone is not enough – learning is also important. If supply chains wish to become more resistant to disruptions, they must be more dynamic, intelligent and better infrastructure-equipped. Thanks to this approach, companies operating in the resilient structures of supply chains may experience a transition to a higher level of initiation.

References

Allam Z. (2020). *Surveying the COVID-19 Pandemic and Its Implications: Urban Health, Data Technology and Political Economy*. London: Elsevier.

Bozarth C.B. and Handfield R.B. (2021). *Introduction to Operations and Supply Chain Management: Global Edition*, 4th Edition. London: Pearson Education Limited.

Chetan K. and Yogish S.N. (2020). "Global economy with comparative study of India and China in a pandemic situation". *International Research Journal on Advanced Science Hub* 2(10), 1–5.

Christopher M. and Peck H. (2004). "Building the resilient supply chain". *International Journal of Logistics Management* 15(2), 1–14.

Coveri A., Cozza C., Nascia L. and Zanfei A. (2020). "Supply chain contagion and role of industrial policy". *Journal of Industrial and Business Economics* 47, 467–482.

Gryz J. and Kitler W. (2007). *System reagowania kryzysowego*. Toruń: Wydawnictwo Adam Marszałek.

Guan D., Wang D., Hallegatte S., Huo J., Li S., Bai Y., Lei T., Xue Q., Davis S.J., Coffman D., Cheng D., Chen P., Liang X., Xu B., Lu X., Wang S., Hubacek K. and Gong P. (2020). "Global economic footprint of the COVID-19 pandemic". *Research Square*, 28 April.

Harland C., Lamming R., Walker H., Caldwell N., Johnsen T.E. et al. (2006). "Supply management: Is it a discipline?". *International Journal of Operations & Production Management* 26(7), 730–753. https://doi.org/10.1108/01443570610672211.

Harrison A. and Hoek R. (2010). *Zarządzanie logistyką*. Warszawa: PWE.

Lee H.L. (2004). "The triple-A supply chain". *Harvard Business Review*, October. Retrieved from https://hbr.org/2004/10/the-triple-a-supply-chain. Accessed: 28.09.2021.

Lee S.M. and Rha J.S. (2026). "Ambidextrous supply chain as a dynamic capability: Building a resilient supply chain". *Management Decision* 54(1), 2–23. https://doi.org/10.1108/MD-12-2014-0674.

Mensah P., Merkuryev Y. and Longo F. (2015). "Using ICT in developing a resilient supply chain strategy". *Procedia Computer Science* 43, 101–108. https://doi.org/10.1016/j.procs.2014.12.014.

Michałowska M., Stankiewicz D. and Danielak W. (2015). "Zarządzanie sytuacją kryzysową w przedsiębiorstwie". *Zeszyty Naukowe PTE w Zielonej Górze* 2, 110–126.

Nepelski M. (2016). *Zarządzanie w sytuacjach kryzysowych*. Szczytno: Wyższa Szkoła Policji w Szczytnie.

Poitiers N. and Weil P. (2021). "A new direction for the European Union's half-hearted semiconductor strategy". *Policy Contribution* 17, Bruegel. https://www.bruegel.org/policy-brief/new-direction-european-unions-half-hearted-semiconductor-strategy. Accessed: 2.06.2021.

Poudel P.B., Poudel M.R., Gautam A., Phuyal S., Tiwari C.K., Bashyal N. and Bashyal S. (2020). "COVID-19 and its global impact on food and agriculture". *Journal of Biology and Today's World* 9(5), 221.

Purvis L., Spall S., Naim M. and Spiegler V. (2016). "Developing a resilient supply chain strategy during 'boom' and 'bust'". *Production Planning & Control* 27(7–8), 579–590. https://doi.org/10.1080/09537287.2016.1165306.

Rezapour S., Zanjirani Farahani R. and Pourakbar M. (2017). "Resilient supply chain network design under competition". *European Journal of Operational Research* 259(3), 1017–1035. https://doi.org/10.1016/j.ejor.2016.11.041.

Saleh Y.D. (2016). *Crisis Management: The Art of Success & Failure*. Maitland: Mill City Press, Inc.

Smoleń K. (2021). "Funkcjonowanie przedsiębiorstw logistycznych w dobie pandemii COVID-19". In: *Transport i łańcuchy dostaw w czasie pandemii*, M. Ziółko and D. Dziedzic (eds.) (131–136). Warszawa: CeDeWu.

Tenerowicz M., "Rynek i logistyka usług kurierskich w obliczu pandemii COVID-19". In: *Transport i łańcuchy dostaw w czasie pandemii*, M. Ziółko and D. Dziedzic (eds.) (23–34). Warszawa: CeDeWu.

Walas-Trębacz J. and Ziarko J. (2010). *Podstawy zarządzania kryzysowego*. Kraków: Krakowska Akademia im. Frycza Modrzewskiego.

Xiling Wu. (2021). "An analysis on the crisis of 'chips shortage' in automobile industry – based on the double influence of COVID-19 and trade friction". *Journal of Physics: Conference Series* 1971.

Zahiri B., Zhuang J. and Mohammadi M. (2017). "Toward an integrated sustainable-resilient supply chain: Transportation research", Part E. *Logistics and Transportation Review* 103, 109–142. https://doi.org/10.1016/j.tre.2017.04.009.

Zakrzewska-Bielawska A. (2008). „Zarządzanie w kryzysie". In: *Zarządzanie ryzykiem operacyjnym*, I. Staniec, J. Zawiła-Niedźwiecki (eds.) (65–92). Warszawa: C.H. Beck.

Zygmunt A., Zygmunt J. (eds.) (2016). *Dostosowanie przedsiębiorstw do zmian otoczenia zewnętrznego*. Opole: Oficyna Wydawnicza Politechniki Opolskiej.

https://www.bankier.pl/wiadomosc/PKB-USA-w-II-kwartale-2021-r-8161355.html. Accessed: 28.09.2021.

https://ec.europa.eu/poland/news/210707_economy_pl. Accessed: 28.09.2021.

https://www.bankier.pl/wiadomosc/Goldman-Sachs-podniosl-prognoze-inflacji-dla-Polski-w-2022-r-8191421.html. Accessed: 28.09.2021.

Tomasz Kafel, Ph.D, Assc. Prof.
Krakow University of Economics

Bernard Ziębicki, Ph.D, Assc. Prof.
Krakow University of Economics

Specifics of formulating the strategy of a higher education institution: A comparative study of the Warsaw University and the Krakow University of Economics (CUE)

Abstract

This chapter aims to present the specific nature of formulating the strategy of a higher education institution, and to perform a comparative analysis of the Warsaw University and the Krakow University of Economics (CUE) in this respect. In the theoretical part, the authors discussed how an institution is managed in view of the challenges of the New Veberist concept. The key scenarios of the development of higher education were also specified. In the research part, the authors described the so-called exploration case study conducted by them, as well as the results of a comparative analysis of the strategic management process at certain entities.

Keywords: higher education institution, strategic management, comparative analysis, cxploration case study, ctrategic initiatives, development strategies

Introduction

The new Act on Higher Education and Science, enacted in 2018, has fundamentally shifted the principles of functioning for the higher education sector in Poland. In the wake of this, these institutions were faced with the need to change their previous strategies as well as their approach to creating them. One priority resulting from the act was research activity, reflected in highly scored publications and projects that generate revenues. The ranking mechanism of evaluating scientific disciplines has caused the need to maximize effects in this regard. As a result, higher education institutions have adopted new strategies, giving priority to the aspects of evaluating scientific disciplines. The process of their operationalization has included various mechanisms of influencing the effect of maximization. These strategies, to a much bigger extent than before, started resembling solutions used in business. The purpose of the chapter is to present the modified approach to creating strategies for higher education institutions caused by the current conditions of the operation of these entities. In order to reflect the contemporary tendencies, the authors will present an analysis of two example institutions where the strategies have been adopted, as well as the approach to strategy creation itself.

Literature review

University management in view of the challenges of the New Weberian Concept

The strategies, and in particular the strategic goals of public higher education institutions, cannot function separated from the public policies being formed in a given country for the higher education sector, or more broadly for public sector management. Seeking methods for improving the effectiveness of the public sector based on the management models applied in the private sector has become a core element in the creation of the New Public Management concept (NPM) since the 1980s (Hood, 1991; Hood and Jackson, 1991 according to Mourato et al., 2019). Since that time, also higher education institution management has seen the increasing use of such criteria as market orientation, effectiveness, result measurement (Ferlie et al., 2008 according to Mourato et al., 2019). Another trend in public management, namely the governance concept, promotes treating stakeholders as partners, rather than clients, and hints that the role played by the government should be mediation instead of control. The dominant scheme in management which covers this concept is a network which is proposed to involve all the parties concerned.

According to this idea, achieving external legitimization is key for the success of a public institution. There are many signs of the implementation of the NPM and the Governance concepts in the strategic management of schools, and these include, first of all: autonomy, responsibility, quality, assessment, leadership, and commitment of external stakeholders in the management process (Mourato et al., 2019).

On the other hand, recent years have seen the development of neo-Weberism (Neo-Weberian State), developed by C. Pollitt and G. Bouckaert (2011). At the foundation of this concept lies Max Weber's public administration model updated by elements of New Public Management and Governance. A neo-Weberian state operates based on eight principles (Oramus, 2016, p. 42). The first four, namely the centrality of the state, reforming and enforcing the administrative law, keeping the public service concept, and representative democracy refer to Max Weber's bureaucratic theory, while the subsequent four, i.e., focusing on the citizens, supplementary public consultations, and direct involvement of citizens, focusing on the results, and professional management, are in line with the NPM and Governance concept.

According to C. Pollitt and G. Bouckaert (2011), the rules listed combine the best elements of the three management concepts, namely Max Weber's bureaucratic theory, the New Public Management concept, and the Governance concept. These concepts should forge a modern state that will function in an efficient and effective way while serving the needs of the citizens. The neo-Weberian state model should thus be reflected in managing higher education entities that are public entities. This applies particularly to the two most recent rules, i.e., focusing on the results, which means the need to modify the management method for the school's resources in such a way that the authorities are held accountable, primarily based on results (rather than compliance with the valid regulations), and the principles of professional management.

Scenarios of development in the higher education sector

The literature devoted to the evolution of the higher education sector has distinguished at least three university models: first generation – based on science, second generation – based on science and research, and third generation – based on science, research, knowledge transfer, and commercialization (Wissema, 2009; Czaja and Kafel, 2021). Source from the recent decade also list the fourth-generation university concept, but its nature is not clearly defined. The authors refer to broadly understood technology, and they identify a fourth-generation university with an entrepreneurial university (Gibb et al., 2009; Czaja and Kafel, 2021), e-university, smart university, cloud university, or a university synchronically cooperating with the Industry 4.0 (Gueye and Exposito, 2020). Close cooperation with the industry and the stakeholders becomes a feature shared between many concepts of modern universities. Furthermore, the technological changes in it require universities to apply advanced technologies, among others artificial intelligence, and to create a virtual environment simulating the conditions in which business entities operate. The university, as an element of the triple (Etzkowitz and Leydesdorff, 1999), quadruple (Kusio, 2019), and even quintuple helix (Carayannis et al., 2012) in the university – industry – government – society – environment system is building an environmentally responsible "social – technical world" (Czaja and Kafel, 2021).

The contemporary universities use abilities created by the digital transformation and consider digital technologies a key development factor. This is of great importance given the current shifts in the structure of the labor market, as well as in employment forms and the ways of working. Digital competences are not only an educational requirement, but the main condition of acquiring knowledge and being recruited on the labor market. According to the authors of the report titled *Poza horyzont – Kurs na edukację. Przyszłość systemu rozwoju kompetencji w Polsce* (Beyond the horizon – Course for Education, Future of the Competence Development System in Poland), the changes faced by the world consist in the absence of patterns, which could be taken over and treated as 'a cheat sheet', later improved and adjusted to local conditions (Czaja and Kafel, 2021). This results, among others, from the fact that it is difficult to specify the exact end of transition in the educational system. Due to the tsunami that is technological advancement, many brick-and-mortar schools are being left in the dust when they remain based on previously developed solutions, and following subsequent "technological revolutions" does not offer great chances in facing new challenges that continue to emerge. The authors of the Report believe that such an educational policy will always be reactive and belated. It is therefore not surprising that alongside scenarios of conservative, free-market, open learning, and global networks, the developmental scenarios for the higher education sector described by them also point to a world of no universities. And most of the research in it shall be carried out by specialized research centers (outside the higher education system). Unfortunately, the authors of the Report are not the only ones to present such pessimistic perspectives, and the best example of that is the thesis presented in the book *The Innovative University: Changing the DNA of Higher Education from the Inside Out*. In this book, the authors claim that in 15 years' time, more than half of the universities will go bankrupt (Christensen and Eyring, 2011). It seems, however, that the current changes at Polish universities indicate a dominant scenario in the form of a hybrid between open learning and global networks (Czaja and Kafel, 2021). The most typical features of this vision will probably include:

1) strong integration between universities and the economy both in the sphere of scientific research and educating competent employees,
2) more external financing for education and scientific research,
3) intensified cooperation between universities and their stakeholders as per the assumptions of the sharing economy,
4) individual education models designed by students in the network of global higher education institutions,
5) some universities opening on educating students at the cost of scientific research (Czaja and Kafel, 2021).

Strategic management of a public higher education institution

The specific nature of the strategic management of a public higher education school is determined particularly by its surroundings, which cover a broad range of organizations. At this point, it is difficult to distinguish its homogeneous elements. There is certainly a presence of such pressure forces as the government, taxpayers, donors, as well as the sponsors, students, and competition. The strategies of a public higher education institution are often created with an extensive participation of their stakeholders; they are open, discussed publicly, and subject to public evaluation.[2] According to A. Witek-Crabb, the most important issues that shape strategic management in a non-profit organization – and those include public higher education schools – are interpretation of the mission and values, the goals, the results, the clients, and the competition. Public higher education institutions do not act based on any financial motivation, which does not exclude achieving profits. They go beyond putting emphasis on business and center around the mission, sense of a common goal, and joint service. Public higher education schools struggle to specify objectives clearly and qualitatively, as well as to measure the results and efficiency, and the basic reason is the intangible nature of their operations. The products are often intangible, difficult to capture, and they comprise a social benefit in nature. An additional difficulty in determining goals at public higher education schools unambiguously is posed by the numerous group of stakeholders who affect the directions and decisions taken by the organization; often times, their interests are different or even contradictory. A public higher education school has several different groups of customers (or recipients). Adrian Sargeant mentions two basic groups – donors and beneficial owners. This also determines the specific operational nature of a higher education school. Here, the acquisition of resources and their allocation are separated. In other words, an organization offers its services to beneficiaries, while it receives resources (specifically, 'payment' for these services) from donors. Therefore, transactions are not bidirectional as in the business (an exchange of products and money with the client) but involve a certain "flow" – a public higher education school distributes resources (money, items, work) that it has acquired earlier. Thus, the organization's suppliers are also its customers. In a way, this reality enforces a certain competition for limited resources and goods between higher education schools. Whether they like it or not, they compete for funds, employees, influence, as well as prestige, connections, and orders, recipients, and users, and sometimes also for tp. he members of Councils (Greenberg, 1982, p. 82). However, the main problem

---

[2]   A much bigger similarity can be seen between the strategic behaviors and conditions of shaping the strategies of NGO and public institutions than in the case of enterprises, therefore, the non-governmental sector and the public sector are often discussed jointly (Prawelska-Skrzypek, 2006).

in specifying strategic goals at public higher education schools is comparing the benefits, the costs, and the risks associated with the implementation of actions or projects. It is also difficult to measure the execution level of tasks and the lack of clarity regarding the responsibility taken for decisions.

We can distinguish four basic benefits of strategic management at public higher education schools:

1) strategic management constitutes an intellectual platform between institutions that fund services and their recipients, the essence of which is the discipline that is necessary to evaluate the needs of the users, organize resources (which allow to fulfill those needs), and control the results,

2) by creating frameworks which make it possible to balance various opinions in order to create a shared vision of a school's future, strategic management constitutes a mechanism for building a coalition focused on new priorities,

3) strategic management facilitates the development of a new concept of a school's identity and the verification of the goal which it serves. This involves schools' growing freedom in shaping its strategy, which is why they frequently diversify their goals,

4) strategic management is used to maintain or to extend the scope of the school's independence in relation to the increased participation of financing institutions in their financial structure (Kafel, 2014).

Research method

This study comprises an attempt to compare the process of preparing a strategy in a higher education institution, and to indicate good practices in this respect. The research strategy based on a case study was chosen for several reasons. The starting point was the ability to use specified theoretical frameworks in the research process, in this case the concept of strategic management. An extremely significant premise for the selection of the case study method was the ability to test the research model, and, consequently, not only to better understand the mutual relation factors specified, but also to modify and supplement the cognitive gaps indicated, and to improve the theory (Ćwiklicki and Pilch, 2018; Haller and Stott, 2010). The choice was also justified by the fact that the case study method may include various epistemological orientations and makes it possible to merge both quantitative and qualitative research techniques (Ćwiklicki and Pilch, 2018). A further circumstance supporting this choice was also the ability to use it to prepare practical solutions (Matejun, 2012). The authors used the exploration case study model, which makes it possible to initially identify the subject of the examination and to formulate the issues and strategy for future research (Yin, 2015). The analysis also has the nature of the so-called instrumental case study, which serves the auxiliary role, i.e., it is selected, since it constitutes an illustration of an issue that is important from the researcher's point of view (Mizerek, 2017). Here, several points of views are applied, and the consideration of theoretical perspectives makes it possible to understand the studied problem. We can recognize the application of the so-called evaluation approach aimed at, first and foremost, "determining the value of the program or the project that determines the case being considered." The adopted axiological perspective is of major significance, since it is used as the basis for the researcher to define the extent to which the study subject implements the values assumed, after which the scientist must publish their findings (Mizerek, 2017). The steps taken in this study have been determined according to the case analysis methodology proposed by W. Czakon (2006), and they include the following stages: defining the survey questions, selecting the cases, selecting the data gathering tools, gathering the data, data analysis, shaping the generalizations, confronting the results with the literature, formulating the generalizations. The key question posed was: Are there common characteristics in the development strategies developed by the Warsaw University and the Krakow University of Economics (if yes, what are they?). The study was purposefully limited to two entities, since this increased the chance to use the data triangulation method by accessing documents, participatory observations, and own experience. The theoretical layer was prepared by examining secondary sources: previous studies and analyses, governmental documents, and articles related to the concept of university strategic management, published in both domestic and foreign academic journals. This study covered an extensive literature review, where the present state and perspectives of knowledge were critically analyzed.

Results and discussion

Strategy of the Warsaw University: Development process and content

The Warsaw University (UW) has adopted six strategic initiatives, which include:

- "Excellence Initiative – Research University" program,
- 4EU + Alliance, which has received the status of a European university in the European Commission competition "European Universities",
- Multi-year program "Warsaw University 2016–2025", which covers 18 investments intended to create proper conditions for the university's development,
- Program of integrated activities for the development of UW – ZIP used to finance the implementation of measures for increasing the education quality, enriching the educational offer, and developing student and employee competence,
- International research programs (the European Union's Knowledge and Innovation Associations, International Research Agendas),
- Federalization with the Warsaw Medical University (Excellence Initiative – Research University at the Warsaw University).

The implementation of the 6 strategic programs mentioned above by the Warsaw University is intended, first, to: strengthen UW's position as the best research center in Poland, to maintain a high rank among Central and Eastern Europe universities, and to bring together the leaders of the higher education institutions on the continent, as well as to achieve international recognizability and strengthen the effect on the environment, in particular by undertaking socially important research topics.

One of the premises for choosing the University of Warsaw as the subject matter of this case analysis was the fact that UW was ranked 1 in the "Excellence Initiative – Research University" contest of the Ministry of Science and Higher Education (IDUB). By winning the competition, in 2020–2026 UW will receive a subsidy increased by 10% (more than PLN 72 million). The IDUB program will encompass two types of activities which will take place at UW: operations assigned to priority research areas and general university activities. The process of preparing a request within the competition involved the need to conduct a strategic analysis and to choose strategic goals for UW. The competition requirements involved the need to define the so-called Priority Research Areas (POB) in the fields of UW's scientific activities. Strategic analysis involved the use of the SWOT – TOWS method based, among others, on the assumptions described by Robert G. Dyson in the paper "Strategic development and SWOT analysis at the University of Warwick". Dyson perceived it as a possibility of connecting in strategy design an attitude based on resources and competences with scenario analysis, while rejecting criticism indicating its obsolescence. The stages of strategy formulation according to Robert G. Dyson, adopted to a great extent by UW, are presented in Figure 1.

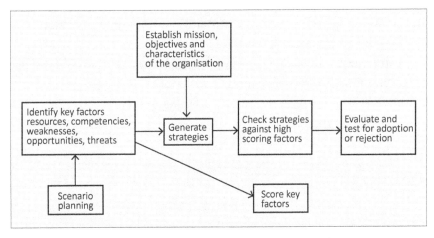

Figure 1. Strategy formulation process according to Robert G. Dyson

Source: R.G. Dyson (2004). "Strategic development and SWOT analysis at the University of Warwick". *European Journal of Operational Research* 152, p. 638.

The starting point in the strategy development process for UW was to identify the expectations of the University's stakeholders, and in particular of the key stakeholder, namely the Ministry of Science and Higher Education. Among these expectations, the following have been highlighted: increasing the impact on global science, strengthening cooperation with world-renowned scientific facilities, improving the quality of educating students and doctoral candidates (among others, including them in research activities), and competing for talented candidates (including from abroad), as well as professional development of employees (young people), bettering the quality of the university's governance and management (SWOT analysis for the "Excellence Initiative – Research University" program, 2020). As part of the first step of strategy design, a commission formed by representatives of all the scientific fields at UW identified the internal factors (key success factors) and external factors that comprised the requirements for achieving these goals. Next, these factors were referred to UW's resources and its status in the context of other schools and academic facilities, which made it possible to define UW's comparative advantages, weaknesses, as well as opportunities and threats. The factors specified were assigned weights and ranks, allowing to reduce the list down to the five-seven most important elements. The collection presented in Table 1 demonstrates the factors which have received the maximum index value (the product of the weight and the rank) according to the commission.

Table 1. SWOT Analysis for the Warsaw University

Strengths	Weaknesses
Research communities, programs, and projects with big potential of internationalizing and achieving significant scientific results.	Poorly prepared for the intensive mobility of internationalization.
	Relatively weaker scientific disciplines.
Well-functioning partner relations with world-renowned scientific facilities.	No effective management system for knowledge, research infrastructure, and academic activities.
Modern research infrastructure and unique scientific resources.	
Scientific disciplines with a high development potential and significant impact on the global science (ranking high in rankings).	Insufficient support for employees in conducting scientific and teaching operations.

Strengths	Weaknesses
Education programs, which have received international certificates. Globally renowned scientists, outstanding young scientists. Most effective in Poland in acquiring grants. Location in Warsaw, and in the region of Central and Eastern Europe.	No consistent and transparent management policy for human resource in employee development. Insufficiently prepared for internal cooperation building relations with stakeholders.

Opportunities	Threats
Federalization with the Warsaw Medical University Participation in the European Research Schools Alliance 4EU +. New scientific-research policy of the state. Synergy of change and development programs implemented at UW. HR Excellence in research and human resources management. Increasing demand for expert analyses and research.	UW's lowering or not improving position in international rankings. Leaving employees. Western universities attracting talented youth from Poland (universities offering mass open online classes the so-called MOOC). Higher costs of investing in and maintaining the infrastructure. Moderate innovativeness of Poland.

Source: study based on the SWOT analysis for the "Excellence Initiative – Research University" program, 2020.

The SWOT analysis revealed a diversified and scattered potential of UW in the scope of science and education, as well as material resources. Further analytical proceedings in line with the SWOT – TOWS method recognized that the best strategy for UW will be competitive (aggressive), whereby the foundation is to use (*leverage*) the strengths and opportunities in order to remove or minimize the weaknesses and threats. Such an approach served to ensure the lasting effect of the mechanisms and processes activated. Based on the SWOT analysis and the assumption of this very strategy, priority research areas were also identified, and a package of development-oriented activities was prepared. The choice of priority research areas (POW) and determination of operational objectives proceeded in line with applying the ideas of leveraging, scaling, and strengthening the knowledge and innovation spillover effects in the process of designing POW; account was also taken of adding new elements to the excellence islands at UW, strong scientific disciplines and environments, as well as synergistic combination of resources. It should be emphasized that the priority research areas at UW, presented in Tab. 1, were identified using the following three criteria:

- ◆ associating strong research disciplines with relatively weaker ones,
- ◆ the multi-field nature of the research (it had to be determined whether the research area helps in solving fundamental problems in science and social challenges – where these very associations are necessary, e.g., studying threats to the natural environment requires combination of the disciplines which are on the world's highest level at UW (Physics, Chemistry), and slightly weaker disciplines (e.g., Biology),
- ◆ involving international and research teams and communities operating at UW that have a high development potential and good networking with world-renowned foreign centers which have already worked in this kind of research areas.

Table 2. Priority research areas of Warsaw University

Priority name	Strong fields	Internationalized teams and communities	Significance for the stakeholders
Research for the Earth. Integrated multidisciplinary approach for identifying threats to the natural environment, biodiversity, climate, and health, as well as looking for feasible solutions.	Physics, Chemistry, Earth sciences (adding Medicine, which is necessary in this area - necessary Federalization with the Warsaw Medical University)	Department of Physics, EIT Food, EIT Climate	Priority in the UN and EU agenda (Action for the Planet)
At the basis of the micro- and macro world. Seeking breakthrough innovations for the future: materials, energy sources, and technologies that ensure sustainable development.	Astronomy, Chemistry, Physics	Quantum Optical Technologies Center	Priority in the agenda of international organizations, governments, manufacturing industry

Priority name	Strong fields	Internationalized teams and communities	Significance for the stakeholders
Petabyte challenge. Tools for advanced mathematics and information technology in analyzing large data sets – from random processes on stock exchanges to medical diagnostics.	Mathematics, IT, Physics	Department of Mathematics, IT, and Mechanic (ERC grants), Digital Economy Lab	Priority in the EU and World Economic Forum agenda
Expanding the boundaries of the humanities. Humanistic research exceeding the limits of disciplines that develop innovative tools and models, go beyond the understanding of the mind, language, and culture.	Philosophy, Archeology, Psychology; unique disciplines and specialties	DARIAH-PL, Artes Liberales Department (2 ERC grants), Laboratorium Medioznawcze, Baby Lab	Priority in the EU agenda (among others, preflagship Time Machine in digital humanities)
In searching for regional solutions for global challenges. Multidisciplinary teams that study the consequences of increasing mobility, multidimensional inequalities, and digital transformation.	Economy, Geography, Political science	Migrations Research Center, Institute of Social Sciences	Priority in the agenda of most international organizations

Source: own study on the basis of: Analiza SWOT na potrzeby programu "Inicjatywa doskonałości – uczelnia badawcza", 2020, pp. 63–66.

It should be mentioned that the Priority Research Areas listed have been developed with the participation of strategic teams working at the SWOT, which includes representatives of all the disciplines and organizational units at UW. Importantly, these teams have filled each POB with content during the preparation of the research agenda and the action plan. Based on the activities worked out by the POB teams, and after consultations with the UW authorities, including the key administrative entities, a set of specific objectives was created (Analiza SWOT na potrzeby programu "Inicjatywa doskonałości – uczelnia badawcza", 2020, pp. 63–66). The projects are selected, namely approved for financing or co-financing, in order to accomplish specific objectives within POB, under two types of competitions:

- continuous, e.g., for micro-grants,
- periodical (organized at least twice a year), e.g., for mobility projects or for support for journals.

It is worth noting that in order to describe the discussed projects, the authors must not only characterize the actions taken, but also: determine the budget for an activity, specify funding sources other than IDUB, specify the milestones within the activity implementation process, define the indicators for the effects, as well as determine units to coordinate the activity. The structure of the document used in the project selection process together with complete requirements is presented in Figure 2.

Activity no. based on the application	Activity title
IDUB goal achievement	
Name of POB/ Activity Group	

Activity description (up to 1000 words)	Objectives Substantiation				
	Tasks or projects within the tasks				
Activity budget	Total	2020	2021	2022	2023
Financing sources other than IDUB	Yes/No (if yes, please indicate what they are)				
Milestones		2020	2021	2022	2023
Required and voluntary result indicators					
Action coordinating unit					
Entities involved in activity implementation					
Activity coordinator					

Figure 2. Information required in the assessment and selection of projects under IDUB at UW

Source: "Excellence Initiative – Research University". Presentation at the meeting of the Senate of the Warsaw University on January 22, 2020. Maciej Duszczyk – Vice-president for Science.

The implementation of the activities related to introducing POB is co-ordinated by the Coordinating Committee of five Priority Research Areas which is directly subordinated to the Vice-Rector for Science. This Committee consists of 15 persons, 3 individuals from each POB, and all the Departments and other entities of the Warsaw University have appointed coordinators for the project "Excellence Initiative – Research University" (Figure 3).

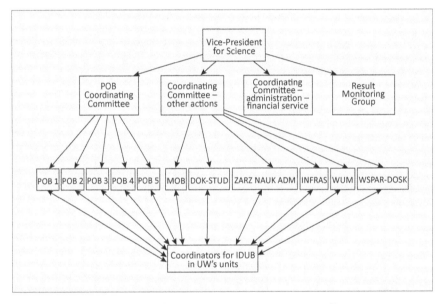

Figure 3. Coordination of project implementation. "Excellence Initiative – Research University" at other entities of Warsaw University

OB coordinating committee – 15 persons (3 individuals from each POB)

Coordinating committee OTHER ACTIONS – managers of the central administration offices and one person from each KK IDUB (POB, ADM-FIN, MONIT)

Administration-finance coordinating committee – representatives of the Chancellor, the Bursar, deputies of the Chancellor for economic affairs. BOB Manager, BMPB Manager, BWR Manager, ZIP Manager, Multi-Year Plan Manager. IDUB Coordinator.

Results monitoring group – people involved in positioning UW in rankings.

Coordinators for IDUB in UW units – appointed at the UW departments and other units to coordinate the implementation of IDUB projects.

Source: "Excellence Initiative – Research University". Presentation at the meeting of the Senate of the Warsaw University of January 22, 2020. Maciej Duszczyk – Vice-president for Science.

Strategy of the Krakow University of Economics (CUE): Development process and content

In 2021 Krakow University of Economics has prepared a new development strategy and implemented it for the years 2021–2024. This vision differs substantially from the previous ones. The two preceding strategies were concerned with a ten-years perspective (strategies for 2001–2010 and 2011–2020), while the current one covers four years. The differences between the current plan and the preceding ones are also related to other aspects. The core focus of the preceding strategies was the didactic process, meanwhile the present strategy centers around scientific operations. The earlier strategies have also been characterized with a significantly higher generality of goals. They involved was no responsibility for the implementation of the goals assigned, and these goals were not associated with any detailed cost analysis, as well as there were no mechanisms for current evaluation of the effects. The differences are listed in the table below (Table 3).

Table 3. UEK strategies over the last 20 years

	Strategy 2001–2010	**Strategy 2011–2020**	**Strategy 2021–2024**
Timeframe	10 years	10 years	4 years
Key focus	didactic process	didactic process	scientific activities
Level of detail	medium	medium	high
Responsibility	scattered	scattered	assigned, clear
Cost analysis	none	general	detailed
Implementation current assessment	none	none	monitoring system

Source: prepared by the authors.

Operationalizing the UEK strategy 2011–2024 includes 8 key programs:
- scientific excellence (Vice Chancellor for Science),
- high quality education (Vice-Rector for Education and Students),
- active and responsible UEK (Prorector for Projects and Cooperation),
- modern employer (Director of the Rector's Office),
- a strong brand (Director of the Brand and Communications Department),
- modern campus (Director of the Department of Resources and Development),
- financial stability (Director of the Department of Finance and Procurement),
- digital university (Director of Information Technology – Rector's Representative).

The responsibility for implementing these programs has been assigned to the Vice Rectors and the Heads of Divisions. Within particular key programs, detailed tasks (projects) have been specified. Each task involves a project implementation matrix (Figure 4), in which the following have been specified: responsibility for the task, task characteristics, task objectives, expected task results (expressed by the implementation measures and indicators), and the schedule of works and expenditures, which covers: activities within the task, implementation time, and costs. Each task is approved by the Vice-President or the Department Director and the Chief Financial Officer. The competent Vice-President or the Head of Division is responsible for the coordination, substantive and managerial supervision, as well as first level monitoring of tasks. Current monitoring of the implementation of the key programs is managed by a dedicated organizational unit specifically established for this purpose at UEK. Implementation of the UEK Development Strategy is an ongoing task, carried out using an approved and transparent monitoring system. Monitoring activities take place at four levels (outlined above) and additionally through a satisfaction survey on a semi-annual and/or annual basis (depending on the group surveyed).

The strategy model for the years 2021–2024 adopted at the Krakow University of Economics enables continuous evaluation of the fulfillment of goals. A significant issue in this respect involves measuring progress by employing various measures adapted to the specificity of the area. Given the barely four-year time frame of the adopted strategy, this solution comprises the key determinant for success in the implementation of the adopted objectives.

Key program:	
Task:	
Task coordinator:	
Description:	
Scope:	
Goals:	
Results (expressed by implementation measures and indicators):	

Schedule of Works and Expenditures			
Action	Completion time	Cost	Comments

Confirmation	
Vice-president/Department director	Chief Financial Officer

Figure 4. Project matrix

Source: Development Strategy of the Krakow University of Economics (CUE) 2021–2024.

Conclusion

Among the recommendations for the modernization of Polish higher education, in addition to increasing funding, diversity, improving quality, internationalization, introduction of modern educational methods, consolidation, cooperation with business, strategic management is also mentioned (Olechnicka et al., 2010). The authors believe that the solutions used during preparation of the UW strategy for the needs of the "Excellence Initiative – Research University" program may prove useful in other higher education entities. Special attention should be paid to the process of choosing Priority Research Areas, as well as the designed mechanisms of their implementation and coordination, which may be treated (and are treated as such at UW) as a flywheel in the whole school's qualitative leap. According to the authors of the described and implemented instruments, not only will they create new tools and standards for supporting scientific excellence, but they will also make it possible to activate innovative organizational solutions by using the leveraging strategy element to introduce other organizational modifications. This may help re-scale the existing research and scientific "bridgeheads" and provide a developmental impulse for relatively weaker fields, which could adapt good practices and standards from the strongest ones and allow to achieve an organizational effectiveness comparable to those of their own.

In many aspects, the strategy of the Krakow University of Economics for the years 2021–2024 may also be an example of a benchmark solution. Of particular interest in this case are the operationalizing process as well as current monitoring of the attainment goals based on measurements of the results.

The presented exemplary strategies are characterized by a number of common aspects, which could be treated as general contemporary tendencies in the approach to strategic management at higher education schools in Poland. They apply to the following components: reducing the time, prevailing focus on academic activities, intensified cooperation with the social-economic environment, transparent responsibility, crystallization of tasks, current monitoring and measurement of the results. However, confirmation of the presented hypotheses requires studies which would cover a representative group of both public and private schools.

References

Analiza SWOT na potrzeby programu „Inicjatywa doskonałości – uczelnia badawcza". (2020). https://www.uw.edu.pl/badania/idub/. Accessed: 5.02.2021.

Carayannis E.G., Barth T.D. and Campbell D.F. (2012). "The Quintuple Helix innovation model: Global warming as a challenge and driver for innovation". *Journal of Innovation and Entrepreneurship* 1, 2. https://doi.org/10.1186/2192-5372-1-2.

Christensen C.M. and Eyring H.J. (2011). *The Innovative University: Changing the DNA of Higher Education*. Hoboken: John Wiley & Sons.

Czaja I. and Kafel T. (2021). "Transformacja cyfrowa przedsiębiorczego uniwersytetu". *Przedsiębiorczość – Edukacja* 17(2), 151–163. https://doi.org/10.24917/20833296.172.11.

Czakon W. (2006). "Łabędzie Poppera – *case studies* w badaniach nauk o zarządzaniu". *Przegląd Organizacji* 9, 9–12.

Ćwiklicki M. and Pilch K. (2018). "Rygor metodologiczny wielokrotnego studium przypadku w badaniach marketingu miejsc". *Studia Ekonomiczne. Zeszyty Naukowe Uniwersytetu Ekonomicznego w Katowicach* 376, 23–35.

Dyson R.G. (2004). "Strategic development and SWOT analysis at the University of Warwick". *European Journal of Operational Research* 152, 631–640.

Etzkowitz H. and Leydesdorff L. (1999). "The future location of research and technology transfer". *The Journal of Technology Transfer* 24 (2–3), 111–123.

Ferlie E., Musselin C. and Andresani G. (2008). "The steering of higher education systems: A Public management perspective". *Higher Education* 56, 325–348. https://doi.org/10.1007/s10734-008-9125-5.

Gibb A., Haskins G., Hannon P. and Robertson I. (2009). *Leading the Entrepreneurial University: Meeting the entrepreneurial development needs of higher education institutions*. The National Centre for Entrepreneurship in Education (NCEE), Saïd Business School, Oxford University, 54. https://core.ac.uk/download/pdf/288287534.pdf. Accessed: 15.03.2021.

Greenberg E. (1982). "Competing for scarce resources". *Journal of Business Strategy* 2(3), 82.

Gueye M. and Exposito E. (2020). "University 4.0: The Industry 4.0 paradigm applied to Education". Paper presented at the IX Congreso Nacional de Tecnologías en la Educación, October 2020, Puebla (Mexico), France.

Haller E. and Stott L. (2010). *Studium przypadku – poradnik*. Warszawa: Wydawnictwo Spektrum.

Hood C. (1991). "A public management for all seasons?". *Public Administration* 69, 3–19. https://doi.org/10.1111/j.1467-9299.1991.tb00779.x.

Hood C. and Jackson M. (1991). *Administrati e Argument*. Aldershot: Dartmouth.

Inicjatywa Doskonałości – Uczelnia Badawcza na Uniwersytecie Warszawskim. (n.d.). https://www.uw.edu.pl/inicjatywy-strategiczne-uniwersytetu-warszawskiego/. Accessed: 7.04.2021.

Inicjatywa Doskonałości – Uczelnia Badawcza. (2020). Prezentacja na posiedzeniu Senatu Uniwersytetu Warszawskiego 22 stycznia 2020 roku Maciej Duszczyk – Prorektor ds. naukowych. https://www.uw.edu.pl/badania/idub/ Accessed: 7.04.2021.

Kafel T. (2014). *Metody profesjonalizacji organizacji pozarządowych*. Kraków: Uniwersytet Ekonomiczny w Krakowie.

Kusio T. (2019). *Więzi relacyjne uczelni z biznesem*. Kraków: Wydawnictwo Akademii Górniczo-Hutniczej w Krakowie.

Matejun M. (2012). "Metoda studium przypadku – egzemplifikacja wykorzystania w naukach o zarządzaniu". *Studia Ekonomiczne Regionu Łódzkiego* 7, 349–366.

Mizerek H. (2017). *Studium przypadku w badaniach nad edukacją. Istota i paleta zastosowań*. Olsztyn: Uniwersytet Warmińsko-Mazurski.

Mourato J., Patrício M.T., Loures L. and Morgado H. (2019). "Strategic priorities of Portuguese higher education institutions". *Studies in Higher Education* 46(2), 215–227. https://doi.org/10.1080/03075079.2019.1628202.

Olechnicka A., Pander W., Płoszaj A. and Wojnar K. (2010). *Analiza strategii, modeli działania oraz ścieżek ewolucji wiodących szkół wyższych na świecie. Raport z badania*. Warszawa: Politechnika Warszawska.

Oramus M. (2016). "Neoweberowskie Państwo w kontekście globalnego kryzysu ekonomicznego". *Myśl Ekonomiczna i Polityczna* 1(52), 42.

Pollitt Ch., Bouckaert G. (2011). *Public Management Reform: A Comparative Analysis – New Public Managemant, Governance, and the Neo-Weberian State*. Oxford: Oxford University Press.

Prawelska-Skrzypek G. (2006). *Zarządzanie w sektorze publicznym i obywatelskim. Wybrane problemy*. Kraków: Fundacja Współczesne Zarządzanie, Instytut Spraw Publicznych UJ.

Uniwersytet Ekonomiczny w Krakowie (2021). "Strategia rozwoju Uniwersytetu Ekonomicznego w Krakowie 2021-2024".

Wissema J.G. (2009). *Towards the Third Generation University: Managing the University in Transition*. Cheltenham: Edward Elgar Publishing.

Yin R.K. (2015). *Studium przypadku w badaniach naukowych: projektowanie i metody*. Kraków: Wydawnictwo UJ.

Jakub Kwaśny, PhD
Krakow University of Economics

Challenges for the development of e-services in local governments

Abstract

The aim of the paper is to outline the concept of e-services and to explain the challenges of e-government solutions, then to present the public e-services model with examples of applied tools and solutions in local government units and an attempt to assess the possible benefits of its implementation in the managerial decision making at local level. Technological advances, new ICT tools and the Internet of Things, as well as the opportunities provided today by the acquisition of big data, mean that management at the local level can be not only simpler but also more efficient. Combining this data and analyzing it in a proper manner through smart solutions can help to identify problems, possible improvements but also to forecast trends for better service delivery. Smart cities, and by extension smart local managers, are already using these tools today. Smart solutions are employed not only for electoral purposes but above all to optimize energy consumption, improve the management of public assets, and to streamline public services. Nevertheless, these changes require effective leadership at the local level. A haphazard approach to harnessing the benefits of the internet revolution causes issues with interoperability for the implemented systems, and results in the dispersion of large quantities of data across different databases; furthermore, it degrades the quality of the provided information. In the wake of this fact, successful implementation of smart and e-government solutions requires effective leadership and a thorough strategy. It is not only a challenge of the present day, but also an inescapable necessity.

Keywords: public management, e-government, local government, ICT, smart city, smart management

Introduction

The emergence of modern techniques and new communication tools, most notably the internet, has revolutionized the approach to delivering public services and communicating with stakeholders. New communication channels have given rise to the so-called social media, as well as useful applications, shopping platforms, e-commerce, e-banking, elaborate websites, e-mail, etc. This clearly demonstrates an awareness about the benefits of transferring more elements of the business into virtual space. The whole process has been accelerated since it has become a necessity as a result of the COVID-19 restrictions. There have also been a number of transformations in the public sector, for which the development of e-services has been an opportunity not only to improve civic awareness and build an information society, but also to increase management efficiency, minimize costs and create a better image overall. The opportunities presented by e-government have made it more accessible in the era of COVID-19 and drastically reduced the need for citizens to visit various offices. Social isolation and constraints have triggered a greater interest in alternative ways of communicating with the office – and thus in making decisions – on both the demand side (citizens) and the supply side (public administration).

Smart city – smart management

Technological advances and the development of ICT have forced organizations to reach for innovative solutions concerning service delivery as well as the use of data, the optimization of services, and decision-making (Buła et al., 2013). E-government entails comprehensive measures; it comprises an important factor in the development of smart cities and represents an area of interest both for academics and policy makers (Pereira et al., 2018). There prevails a general consensus in the literature that the development of e-government accelerates the implementation of smart city solutions (Lytras and Serban, 2020) and that it is necessary to transform the model of the city and urban development in a more competitive and sustainable direction, including, in particular, to improve the attractiveness of administration as we know it (Clark et al., 2015). It is important from the perspective of a city's competitiveness to recognize changes in society and to respond to them quickly. This can help greatly simplify management in public entities and facilitate decision-making. Globalization offers an opportunity for cities not only to automate repetitive processes but also to monitor, analyze, understand and improve them, thereby increasing the quality, efficiency and accessibility of services. However, this requires both long-term and short-term efforts (strategies), a proactive attitude, as well as defining and solving critical problems in an efficient manner (Batty et al., 2012). The emerging market trends and promoted concepts strongly affect the decisions made by managers in enterprises (Kolasińska-Morawska et al., 2022); this is also true for managers in the public sector.

The widespread concept of the 'smart city' is indeed an area of academic interest (Hollands, 2008; Caragliu et al., 2011; Zanella et al. 2014; Chourabi et al., 2012), as well as a major priority for activities funded under the EU cohesion policy (Masik and Studzińska, 2018). Smart city goes far beyond its original understanding as the implementation of sophisticated ICT solutions, with an emphasis on quality of life, including improved economic and environmental conditions (Kourtit and Nijkamp, 2012) and social participation. Smart solutions in cities are therefore a combination of technological and social change. The term smart no longer refers only to modern solutions but also to the very ability of local authorities to manage better and to enrich their public service offerings with innovative solutions for the benefit of the local community (Gonzalez and Rossi, 2011; Traz-Ryan et al., 2011). The opportunities that are within the reach of local governments today go well beyond the previous perception of e-government. Today's solutions allow cities to collect data through a variety of devices and applications, which include transmission and internet networks, utility consumption sensors, video monitoring, use of mobile data. Combining this data and analyzing it by means of smart solutions can help to identify problems, indicate possible improvements, but also to forecast trends for better service delivery (Harrison et al., 2010) taking into account the demand side, which is the citizens themselves (Deloitte, 2015). Thus, smart cities not only use hi-tech solutions, but also collect and process data regarding the population and their habits in order to improve the future quality of services. Importantly, such solutions are usually expensive and their positive effects in the future may not necessarily be an incentive for investment at the initial stage if no external funding is present. Today, smart solutions are used to better the management of public assets, for example in the area of tax collection. New tools helps integrate different systems such as SP, information technology and data communication to meet the needs of local authorities (Chiappini et al., 2020).

E-government makes local managers more efficient

The concept of e-government, which first emerged through A. Gore in 1993 (Gore, 1993), is defined as the provision of public services by means of electronic forms of communication (ICT, information and communications technologies), thereby leading to more efficient public administration (Mulawa, 2013; Hacia, 2013; Dias, 2019). An efficient administration should, first and foremost, connect different social groups, the customers of the e-government, and pursue actions that aim to adapt its services to the existing needs and conditions. The aim of e-government is therefore to improve the quality of life of its 'users', to enhance efficiency, and to make public administration activities more transparent (Snellen, 2002; Pina et al., 2007; Lulewicz, 2013). Both the European Union and the OECD have presented a similar essence of this concept in their documentation, but it is now complemented by organizational changes and new skills introduced by e-government to the public sector, as well as improved democratic processes and transparency (Pina et al., 2009), while also emphasizing increased efficiency (COM, 2003, p. 7; OECD, 2003; Oniszczuk and Rafalski, 2017). The development of digital public administration services is perceived as an opportunity for faster economic development in the EU (Novotny and Sabati, 2007), reduction of administrative operating costs (Haręża, 2011), and streamlined interaction with citizens. Furthermore, the Commission has identified the digital transformation of administrations as a vital element for the success of the single market (COM, 2016; Nowina-Konopka, 2017). Its success, however, requires the exchange of information between various institutions and secure cooperation between different IT systems (Grodzka 2007, p. 2). It is based on interopracticability, which means the ability of varying entities, the ICT systems and public registers which they use, to cooperate in order to achieve mutually beneficial objectives which have been agreed upon by them. This process must also take into account the exchange of information and knowledge, which is a major challenge today – both nationally and in Europe (ISA program) (Banasikowska and Sołtysik-Pierunkiewicz, 2013; Kwaśny, 2013).

The Polish literature draws attention to definitional problems, emphasizing that the mere concept of e-government is broader (Layne and Lee, 2001) than e-government itself, while the English version also encompasses electronic democracy (e-democracy) with systems for e-voting and public participation (Adamczewski et al., 2017; Kaczorowska, 2013; Kwaśny, 2013), at the same time going beyond services provided only by public offices to include subordinate entities such as schools, libraries or public health services. Additionally, despite its common connotation, 'e-government' also implies the use of other forms of communication (not just the internet), from telephone or fax to more advanced technologies such as Bluetooth, GPS, biometrics or mobile payments (Adamczewski et al, 2017). Nevertheless, the most vital element of e-government lies in building relationships with the environment (Ganczar, 2009; Fleszer, 2014), i.e., between the government and the citizens (G2C – government to citizens), the government and the business (G2B – government to business), and between the government offices themselves (G2G – government to government) (Kasprzyk, 2011). This is expected to improve how the administration itself is functioning, but also to ensure that the interests of its customers are considered more strongly (Cohen, 2006).

Proper implementation of e-government solutions allows not only to increase accessibility to public services and make operations more transparent, but also to computerize administration and raise the level of digital literacy. The most common benefits listed include:

◆ improved efficiency of administration (Dixon, 2010) and increased quality of service (Osimo, 2008);

◆ enhanced transparency of operations (Noveck, 2009; Bertot et al., 2010; Chun et al., 2010);

◆ increased interest in public affairs among citizens and facilitated contact with the administration (Lazer et al., 2009);

◆ increased levels of trust in public administration (Bonsón et al., 2012).

There is a perception that the automation of public administration and basing decision-making on algorithms could eliminate traditional bureaucracy in the future (Snellen, 1998), but reality has verified this approach and indicated it only as a way to reduce possible costs (Reddick, 2005).

The most important determinants for the development of local public e-services, which are indicated in the literature, include demographics, socio-economic changes, the level of Internet use, the size of the local government unit, financial capacity, management skills and effective leadership, as well as technical capacity, organizational culture, past experience, social pressure and legal solutions (Dias, 2020). However, a number of case studies highlight the key role of the central government – not only in mobilizing local governments to implement modern solutions, but also to provide adequate funding and technical infrastructure, as well as qualified officials. The role of effective leadership at the local level is also highlighted; problems with the interoperability of implemented systems, which result in a number of data being dispersed across various databases, and the quality of the provided information, including its usability for citizens (Bigdeli et al., 2013; Muksin and Avianto, 2021) as well as for advanced business (Mroczek et al., 2019).

The most important elements on the demand side, which are necessary for the successful implementation of e-solutions, are user-friendliness, compatibility, and reliability. The latter is a key element, but also one that is the most problematic for public administration. After all, it is vital that new solutions are convincing for the citizens (Carter and Bélanger, 2005). However, this is merely the first step in establishing modern public e-services. It is essential to build relationships and to continuously develop and monitor the users. The recommended measures include providing up-to-date and helpful content, increasing the popularity of services, improving the efficiency of communication, and understanding the mutual benefits of using electronic communication tools through feedback (Steyaert, 2004). More attention is now paid to social media and using it to make e-government more effective. In doing so, attention is drawn to the range of benefits which it offers in order to better understand how citizens and business respond to published content and how to reach out to specific social groups (Khasawneh and Abu-Shanab, 2013), networks and clusters more effectively (Kwaśny et al., 2019). Some attention it also given to the role of social media in providing information and countering 'fake news' in times of pandemonium. It is therefore possible that social media could be used to calm sentiment and provide credible information on the spread of the virus (by public health authorities) (Atarodi et al., 2021).

Table 1. E-government scheme with examples

Types of relationships		Levels of e-government					
		administrative				political	smart
		Level 1: information	Level 2: communication	Level 3: services and payments	Level 4: horizontal and vertical integration	Level 5: political participation	Level 6: smart
Internal	official	sharing information online	electronic communication, incl. official letters, questions, requests etc.	transfer of funds, on-line reporting, legal act publications	integrated workflow platform	n.a.	shared services centers
	employee	employee information on salaries, holidays etc.	Intranet, submission of holiday requests etc.	electronic payroll system	integrated employee portal with employee evaluation	n.a.	employee app. with different modules (accounting etc.)

Levels of e-government

Types of relationships		administrative				political	smart
		Level 1: information	Level 2: communication	Level 3: services and payments	Level 4: horizontal and vertical integration	Level 5: political participation	Level 6: smart
External	e-services	public offer description	electronic school enrolment	online payment	e-tickets, residential e-cards	n.a.	integrated app. with access to public services
	political	election calendar	election forms sharing	depositing and accounting for electoral funds	online registration	e-voting	political preferences online monitoring (big data)
	civic	publication of legal acts	online enquiries with public bodies	online broadcasting	integrated citizens information system	online consultations / primary elections	hitizen's preferences online monitoring (big dsta)

Levels of e-government

Types of relationships		Level 1: information	Level 2: communication	Level 3: services and payments	Level 4: horizontal and vertical integration	Level 5: political participation	Level 6: smart
			administrative			**political**	**smart**
External	business	tax information	e-forms, tax services	online payment service	tax and financial reports uploading	online consultations	utility consumption monitoring (water, heat, electricity)
	procurements/contracts	public orders and tender notices	submission of enquires as a part of tender procedures	online payment and reporting	marketplace (online bidding)	n.a.	optimization of public orders
Tools		basic websites, online newsletters	Intranet, e-mails (e.g., Trello)	secure login system platforms	integrated tool from 1.1–3 (and social media)	public trusted profile, e-id	cloud & smart (AI) solutions

Source: own elaboration based on J. Hiller, F. Bélanger (2001). *Privacy Strategies for Electronic Government*, E-government series. Arlington, VA: Pricewaterhouse Coopers Endowment for the business of Government.

Conclusion

Efficient public administration represents a major factor in a country's development, which is why great emphasis has been placed on introducing modern communication techniques in the public sector. The need for multi-channel outreach to the citizen, building networks and cooperation clusters, as well as a growing digital awareness pose further challenges. The development of such services and data sources is supported primarily by the growing benefits, which include:

- saving time, capital and energy of both the official and the citizen,
- increased functionality and efficiency of services,
- increased information – building a civil society,
- transparency of administrative procedures and reduction of corruption,
- improved accessibility of offices,
- providing better data for decision-making,
- increased trust between public managers and business.

Thanks to greater transparency, an efficient and smart e-government, will contribute greatly to reducing corruption and officials' influence on decision-making. More functional services will simplify contact between citizens and the authorities and improve their accessibility. An increased scope of public information and further development of services, including so-called e-participation, will help to build a civil society and increase public awareness. All these arguments speak in favor of expanding the public administration's portfolio of e-services, but it is important to note that they should be understood in the context of three aspects: legal, socio-cultural, and financial. The conditions indicated in the study will help to understand the existing limitations, which may be, on the one hand, an incentive for further development, but on the other hand also a barrier.

References

Adamczewski P., Matusiak J., Mielczarek J., Nowak P.A., Przywojska J. and Szydłowski C. (2017). *Innowacje 2017. Rozwój społeczeństwa informacyjnego w Polsce*. Łódź:

Wydział Społeczeństwa Informacyjnego, Departament Cyfryzacji, Urząd Marszałkowski Województwa Łódzkiego.

Atarodi A., Dastani M., Ghorbani M. and Atarodi A. (2021). "The role of mass media and social media in developing awareness of self-care behavior against the outbreak of Covid-19", *Library Philosophy and Practice* 4848. https://digitalcommons.unl.edu/libphilprac/4848. Accessed: 10.05.2021.

Banasikowska J. and Sołtysik-Piorunkiewicz A. (2013). "Zasady interoperacyjności i standaryzacji w systemach wszechobecnych e-Government krajów Unii Europejskiej". *Roczniki Kolegium Analiz Ekonomicznych* 29, 13–22.

Batty M., Axhausen K., Fosca G., Pozdnoukhov A., Bazzani A. and Wachowicz M. (2012). "Smart cities of the future". *Eur. Phys. J. Special Topics* 214(1), 481–518.

Bertot J.C., Jaeger P.T. and Grimes J.M. (2010). "Using ICTs to create a culture of transparency: E-government and social media as openness and anti-corruption tools for societies". *Government Information Quarterly* 27(3), 264–271. https://doi.org/10.1016/j.giq.2010.03.001.

Bigdeli A.Z., Kamal M.M. and Cesare S. (2013). "Electronic information sharing in local government authorities: Factors influencing the decision-making process". *International Journal of Information Management* 33, 816–830.

Bonsón E., Torres L., Royo S. and Flores F. (2012) "Local e-government 2.0: Social media and corporate transparency in municipalities". *Government Information Quarterly* 29, 123–132.

Buła P., Fudaliński J. and Gorzelany-Dziadkowiec M. (2013). "The concept of integrated management within small and medium-sized enterprises sectors". In: *Management Science in Transition Period in South Africa and Poland*, J. Teczke, N.S. Terblanché (eds.) (313–343). Cracow-Stellenbosch: International Management Foundation, Cracow University of Economics.

Caragliu A., del Bo C. and Nijkamp P. (2011). "Smart cities in Europe". *Journal of Urban Technology* 18(2), 65–82. https://doi.org/10.1080/10630732.2011.601117.

Carter L. and Bélanger F. (2005). "The utilization of e-government services: Citizen trust, innovation and acceptance factors". *Information Systems Journal* 15(1), 5–25. https://doi.org/10.1111/j.1365-2575.2005.00183.x.

Chiappini S., Fini A., Malinverni E.S., Frontoni E., Racioppi G. and Pierdicca R. (2020). "Cost effective spherical photogrammetry: A novel framework for the smart management of complex urban environments". *The International Archives of Photogrammetry, Remote Sensing and Spatial Information Sciences* 43, 441–448.

Chourabi H., Nam T., Walker S., Gil-Garcia J.R., Mellouli S., Nahon K. and Scholl H.J. (2012), "Understanding smart cities: An integrative framework". Paper presented at the *Proceedings of the Annual Hawaii International Conference on System Sciences*, 2289–2297. https://doi.org/10.1109/HICSS.2012.615

Chun S.A., Shulman S., Sandoval R. and Hovy E., (2010). "Government 2.0: Making connections between citizens, data and government". *Information Polity* 15, 1–9.

Clark G., Couturier J., Kelly J. and Moonen T. (2015). *Globalisation and Competition: The New World of Cities*. Chicago, IL, USA: Cities Research Center.

Cohen J.E. (2006). "Citizen satisfaction with contacting government on the Internet". *Information Polity* 11(1), 51–65. https://doi.org/10.3233/ip-2006-0083.

COM (2003). *The Role of eGovernment for Europe's Future*, Communication from the Commission to the Council, the European Parliament, The European Economic and Social Committee and the Committee of the Regions, Bruksela 2003. https://eurlex.europa.eu/LexUriServ/LexUriServ.do?uri=COM: 2003:0567:FIN:EN:PDF. Accessed: 10.01.2021.

COM (2016), *EU eGovernment Action Plan 2016–2020: Accelerating the digital transformation of government*, Communication from the Commission to the Council, the European Parliament, The European Economic and Social Committee and the Committee of the Regions, Bruksela 2016 COM(2016) 179, https://eur-lex.europa.eu/legal-content/EN/TXT/?uri=CELEX%3A52016DC0179. Accessed: 12.01.2021.

Deloitte (2015). *Smart Cities: How Rapid Advances in Technology are Reshaping Our Economy and Society.* https://www2.deloitte.com/tr/en/pages/public-sector/articles/smart-cities.html. Accessed: 10.05.2021.

Dias G.P., (2019), "Fifteen years of e-government research in Ibero-America: A bibliometric analysis". *Government Information Quarterly* 36(3), 400–411. https://doi.org/10.1016/j.giq.2019.05.008.

Dias G.P., (2020), "Determinants of e-government implementation at the local level: An empirical model". *Online Information Review* 44(7), 1307–1326. https://doi.org/10.1108/OIR-04-2020-0148.

Dixon B.E., (2010), "Towards e-government 2.0: An assessment of where e-Government 2.0 is and where it is headed". *Public Administration & Management* 15(2), 418–454.

Fleszer D. (2014). "Wokół problematyki e-administracji". *Roczniki Administracji i Prawa*, 14(11), 125–136.

Ganczar M. (2009). *Informatyzacja administracji publicznej. Nowa jakość usług publicznych dla obywateli i przedsiębiorców*. Warszawa: Wydawnictwo CeDeWu.

Gonzalez J.A., Rossi A. (2011). *New Trends for Smart Cities: Open Innovation Mechanism in Smart Cities*. Brussels: European Commission.

Gore A. (1993). *Creating a Government that Works Better and Costs Less: Reengineering Through Information Technology*. Report of the National Performance Review. Washington DC: Government Printing Office.

Grodzka D. (2007). *E-administracja w Polsce*, no. 18. Warszawa: Infos Biuro Analiz Sejmowych.

Hacia M. (2013). *E-administracja szansą na usprawnienie komunikacji pomiędzy państwem a obywatelem*. In: *E-administracja. Szanse i zagrożenia*, T. Stanisławski, B. Przywora and Ł. Jurek (eds.) (133–144). Lublin: Wydawnictwo KUL.

Haręża A. (2011). "Wprowadzenie do problematyki elektronicznej administracji publicznej". *Prawo Mediów Elektronicznych. Kwartalnik Naukowy* 1, 26–31.

Harrison C., Eckman B., Hamilton R., Hartswick P., Kalagnanam J., Paraszczak J. and Williams P. (2010). "Foundations for smarter cities". *IBM J. Res. Develop.* 54(4), 1–16.

Hiller J. and Bélanger F. (2001). *Privacy strategies for electronic government*. E-government series. Arlington, VA: Pricewaterhouse Coopers Endowment for the business of Government.

Hollands R.G. (2008). "Will the real smart city please stand up? Intelligent, progressive or entrepreneurial?". *City* 12(3), 303–320. https://doi.org/10.1080/13604810802479126.

Kaczorowska A. (2013) *E-usługi administracji publicznej w warunkach zarządzania projektami*. Łódź: Wydawnictwo Uniwersytetu Łódzkiego.

Kasprzyk B. (2011), "Aspekty funkcjonowania e-administracji dla jakości życia obywateli". *Nierówności Społeczne a Wzrost Gospodarczy*, 23, 343–353.

Khasawneh R. T. and Abu-Shanab E. A. (2013). "E-Government and social media sites: The role and impact". *World Journal of Computer Application and Technology* 1(1), 10–17. https://doi.org/10.13189/wjcat.2013.010103.

Kolasińska-Morawska K., Sułkowski Ł., Buła P., Brzozowska M. and Morawski P. (2022). "Smart logistics – sustainable technological innovations in customer service at the last-mile stage: The Polish perspective". *Energies* 15(17), 6395.

Kourtit K. and Nijkamp P. (2012). "Smart cities in the innovation age: Innovation". *The European Journal of Social Sciences* 25(2), 93–95.

Kwaśny J. (2013) "Uwarunkowania rozwoju e-administracji w polskich samorządach". In: *Kultura i administracja w przestrzeni społecznej internetu*, Z. Rykiel, J. Kinal (eds.) (101–116). Rzeszów: Uniwersytet Rzeszowski.

Kwaśny J. (2022). "Rozwój e-administracji w polskich miastach w następstwie kryzysu związanego z pandemią COVID-19". *Horyzonty Polityki* 13(42), 71–90.

Kwaśny J., Mroczek A. and Ulbrych M. (2019). "Industrial clustering and economic performance: In search for evidence from Poland". *Ekonomicko-Manazerske Spektrum*, 13(1), 109–119.

Layne K. and Lee J., (2001). "Developing fully functional e-government: A four stage model". *Government Information Quarterly* 18(2), 122–136. https://doi.org/10.1016/s0740-624x(01)00066-1.

Lazer D., Nebolo M., Esterling K. and Goldschmidt K. (2009). *Online Town Hall Meetings*, Washington, D.C.: Congressional Management Foundation.

Lulewicz E. (2013). *E-administracja – szanse i zagrożenia*. In: *E-administracja. Szanse i zagrożenia*, T. Stanisławski, B. Przywora B. and Ł. Jurek (eds.) (213–224). Lublin: Wydawnictwo KUL.

Lytras M.D. and Serban A.C., (2020). "E-government insights to smart cities research: European Union (EU) study and the role of regulations". *IEEE Access* 8, 65313–65326. https://doi.org/10.1109/access.2020.2982737.

Masik G. and Studzińska D. (2018). "Ewolucja koncepcji i badania miasta inteligentnego". *Przegląd Geograficzny* 90(4), 557–571. https://doi.org/10.7163/PrzG.2018.4.2.

Mroczek A., Kwaśny J. and Ulbrych M. (2019). "The potential of selected Polish cities for attracting advanced business processes". *Studia Miejskie* 36, 57–70. https://doi.org/10.25167/sm.996.

Muksin A. and Avianto B. N. (2021) "Governance innovation: One-stop integrated service to enhance quality service and public satisfaction". *Theoretical and Empirical Researches in Urban Management* 16(1), 40–60.

Mulawa M. (2013). *Wpływ e-administracji na relacje między obywatelem a urzędem – wybrane zagadnienia*. In: *E-administracja. Szanse i zagrożenia*, T. Stanisławski, B. Przywora B. and Ł. Jurek (eds.) (249–264). Lublin: Wydawnictwo KUL.

Nowina-Konopka M. (2017). "Europejska koncepcja e-government w świetle wskaźników Komisji Europejskiej". *Zeszyty Prasoznawcze* 60, 2(230), 329–349. https://doi.org/10.4467/22996362PZ.17.021.7301.

Noveck B. (2009). *Wiki Government: How Technology Can Make Government Better, Democracy Stronger, and Citizens More Powerful*. Washington: Brookings Institution Press.

Novotny D. and Sabati Z. (2007). "Internet enabled public services as a driver of economic growth-case study eCroatia 2006". *Journal of Information and Organizational Sciences* 31(1), 141–156.

OECD (2003). *Implementing e-government in OECD countries: Experiences and challenges,* http://www.oecd. org/ mena /governance/36853121.pdf. Accessed: 12.02.2021.

Oniszczuk D. and Rafalski M. (2017). "E-administracja w Polsce – jak daleko do osiągnięcia poziomu UE". *Ekonomiczne Problemy Usług* 1(126), 2, 385–396. https:// doi.org/10.18276/epu.2017.126/2-38.

Osimo D. (2008). *Web 2.0 in Government: Why and How?* Brussels: European Commission. Joint Research Centre. Institute for Prospective Technological Studies.

Pereira G.V., Parycek P., Falco E. and Kleinhans R. (2018). "Smart governance in the context of smart cities: A literature review". *Information Polity* 23(2), 143–162.

Pina V., Torres L. and Royo S. (2007). "Are ICTs improving transparency and accountability in the EU regional and local governments? An empirical study". *Public Administration* 85(2), 449–472. https://doi.org/ 10.1111/j.1467-9299.2007.00654.x.

Pina V., Torres L. and Royo S. (2009). "E-government evolution in EU local governments: A comparative perspective". *Online Information Review* 33(6), 1137–1168. https://doi.org/10.1108/14684520911011052.

Reddick C.G. (2005). "Citizen interaction with e-government: From the streets to servers?". *Government Information Quaterly* 22, 38–57.

Snellen I. (1998). "Street-level bureaucracy in an information age". In: *Public Administration in an Information Age: A handbook,* I. Snellen and W. van de Donk (eds.) (497–505). Amsterdam: IOS Press.

Snellen I. (2002). "Electronic governance: Implications for citizens, politicians, and public servants". *International Review of Administrative Sciences* 68(2), 183–198.

Steyaert J. C. (2004). "Measuring the performance of electronic government services". *Information & Management* 41, 369–375.

Traz-Ryan B., Velosa A. and Jacobs A. (2011). *Hipe Cycle for Smart City Technologies and Solutions.* Stamford: Gartner.

Zanella A., Bui N., Castellani A., Vangelista L. and Zorzi M. (2014). "Internet of things for smart cities". *IEEE Internet of Things Journal* 1(1), 22–32. https://doi. org/10.1109/JIOT.2014.2306328.

Roman Andrzej Lewandowski, Ph.D, Assc. Prof.
University of Warmia and Mazury in Olsztyn

Measurement and control of physicians' productivity in hospitals

Abstract

In response to increasing costs of treatment, governments have shifted formal responsibility for hospitals from physicians to managers. This has forced the latter to introduce control over clinical activities. Some hospitals go beyond monitoring medical processes merely at the level of wards and delve into the clinical activities of individual doctors. The objective of the study is to identify and understand the manner in which hospital managers have been attempting to implement control over the productivity of individual physicians in relation to their day-to-day clinical practice and how clinicians have been responding to their executive actions. This explorative research was carried out in three Polish public hospitals. We conducted interviews with the hospitals' general managers, medical directors, and physicians. The investigation showed that to some extent, doctors have accepted productivity measures related to the cost of treatment, reimbursement rates, and range of services but at the same time, they have strongly opposed to measurement of the number of patients and the clinical procedures performed by them, especially in the non-surgical department. Managers were unable to engage physicians in the development of quantitative measures which would allow for the objective assessment of their time schedule, even though executives have tried to exploit the conflict between physicians. The defense of professional autonomy concerning clinical workload is given priority by physicians over financial benefits. Physicians have blocked managerial control, simultaneously taking over these methods and incorporating them in self-regulation processes as part of their professional internal assessment. We also found that managers did not focus only on reducing costs while neglecting the quality of treatment, and that clinicians were not solely the intransigent advocates of their autonomy.

Keywords: hospital managers, physician productivity, control measures, professional autonomy, managerial encroachment

Introduction

For decades, healthcare systems have been struggling with rising expenditure. The hospitals in developed countries consume up to 40% of healthcare resources (Eurostat Statistics Explained, 2016). Governments, in order to step up control over the costs of in-patient care, have implemented special methods of payment for medical services, such as the case-mix systems, as well as introduced professional managers into the medical setting and induced competition between hospitals (Miszczyńska and Antczak, 2020; Rüsch, 2016). Medical professionals and managers are both agents 'hired' by the society to protect its welfare. But the society sets contradictory demands: physicians are expected to save patients' health regardless of the costs, while managers are supposed to assure efficiency and productivity. To achieve their goals, clinicians must have knowledge and resources, whereas executives have to exert control over the organization, especially over physicians who are responsible for around 80% of healthcare expenditure (Goes and Zhan, 1995) and may influence hospitals' revenue. Some authors claim that the root of healthcare inefficiency lies in the conflict between physicians and managers. The friction may have originated from physicians' defense of their autonomy (Freidson, 1988) as well as separate fields of interest: the focus of medical professionals mostly centers around quality, whereas managers focus on costs and revenue (Kuhlmann et al., 2011, 2013; Noordegraaf, 2020).

In order to ensure hospitals' sustainability in a competitive environment, managers must reduce costs or/and increase revenue. There is space for that since the cost of treatment and the obtained reimbursement rates for patients with the same conditions treated at the same hospital can vary substantially since different physicians employ a plethora of methods and perform a variety of medical procedures in a time unit (Kaplan and Haas, 2014). Hence, to achieve these objectives managers have to pressure physicians, either by increasing congruency of physicians' and organizational financial goals or tightening control over doctors, or both.

Many Western European countries (e.g.: the UK, Germany, Ireland, and Portugal) have in place national rules concerning physicians' employment and remuneration, preventing managers from implementing payment and bonus systems for a particular hospital. Meanwhile in Poland hospital managers are allowed to create payment and bonus systems for physicians similarly to managers in non-medical private business organizations. This gives Polish managers a wider range of tools that can affect physicians' behavior. Nevertheless, building a control system linking physicians' rewards with the hospital's financial goals in medical settings is difficult because: (1) financial goals may be in conflict with professional ideology and autonomy, and this might evoke physicians' resistance (Freidson, 2001; Lewandowski et al., 2020), (2) contemporary hospitals are often much more complex than companies since they provide very diverse services (e.g. from appendectomy to heart transplantation).

The early literature concerning control of individual physicians' clinical practice has put major emphasis on quality assessment (e.g. Ramsey et al., 1993; Overeem, 2011; Kaye et al., 2014), resource utilization (e.g. Chilingerian and Sherman, 1990) and productivity in ambulatory care (e.g. Checkland et al., 2007; Kantarevic et al., 2011). There are no studies on the productivity of individual physicians in hospitals, although an improvement of physicians' productivity will help not only cut healthcare costs but also alleviate the shortage of physicians (Birch et al., 2009, p. 57). Taking this research gap into account, the main objective of the paper is to identify and understand how hospital managers have been attempting to implement control over individual physicians' productivity in relation to their day-to-day clinical practice and the manner in which the clinicians have responded to executives' actions. The mere question of managers-doctors interaction is not a novelty (Noordegraaf and Abma, 2003), but this research allows to obtain a deeper understanding of particular mechanisms and areas of this interaction.

This study, which sheds more light on the implementation of a measurement system for individual physicians' productivity (MSIPP) in three Polish hospitals that use various methods of payment to physicians, offers an excellent chance to address the above issues and contribute to the existing theory. Furthermore, it entails exciting opportunities – the analysis was carried out in Polish hospitals which have been cut off from the Western public management culture for decades. After the fall of the Iron Curtain, public organizations in Poland were forced to adopt the new public management approach more quickly while disposing of significantly fewer resources than their Western counterparts. This may make it possible to identify phenomena that are less pronounced in Western organizations, and thus more difficult to observe. However, that does not mean that those phenomena are not found there as well. Although the study focuses primarily on Polish hospitals, the findings may also be relevant to healthcare organizations in other countries, especially ones that offer reimbursement of in-patient medical services according to the case-mix payment system.

The following sections encompass a review of the theoretical and empirical literature on professional autonomy and managerial control. Next, we elaborate on the subject of physicians' productivity from the perspective of hospitals. The further part encompasses an explanation of the research methods and the Polish context of healthcare financing. Finally, the paper presents the findings, discussion, conclusions, and the main limitations of the study.

Physicians' autonomy and managerial control

For centuries clinical autonomy has functioned as the defining characteristic of the professional status, power and prestige of physicians (Freidson, 1988; Van-Heuvelen, 2020), and individual practice has been the general standard. According to Abbott (1988), professional autonomy and jurisdiction are based on access to and control over expert knowledge and the possibility of defining the nature and content of the work. This expert and exclusive knowledge does not concern merely codified, abstract know-how accomplished in the course of formal education but also esoteric, unspecified and experiential tacit cognizance obtained in day-to-day practice (Abbott, 1988). Professionalism may be perceived as a system focused on controlling knowledge to gain advantage in the marketplace but also as a structure that supports claims to autonomous work and the exclusive right to an evaluation of medical practice. The medical profession has had its own control model based on self-regulation consisting of a training path, multilevel system of exams, licensing, ethic codes as well as some informal measures, usually specific to workplaces that restrain the assessment of physicians' performance to an unstandardized, subjective and apprenticeship-based model (Van der Vleuten, 1996).

The creation of complex medical organizations (like hospitals) and growing healthcare costs have led governments to shift formal authority for hospital performance from physicians to managers (Doolin, 1999; Abernethy et al., 2006; von Knorring et al., 2010), giving executives organizational power to preside over the whole organizational activity, and especially the revenue and costs. This requires control over the delivery processes of medical services which continue to remain under the jurisdiction of clinicians who are, as before, the only professionals having the legal rights and social legitimization to provide diagnosis and control treatment. This enforced organizational intrusion into the day-to-day clinical practice of physicians is precisely what has evoked conflicts between professional autonomy and hospitals' bureaucracy (Noordegraaf, 2011). However, in many Western countries, managers are significantly restrained from creating payment or bonus schemes for physicians, which stands in contrast to Poland.

Freidson (2001) fails to believe that managers would be able to constrain professional power and autonomy. He claims that managers might allocate resources, but clinicians still remain the end-distributors capable of bypassing managerial decisions through their discretionary powers. Research in Swedish healthcare entities showed that executives perceive their managerial role as weak even though they hold strong formal power and authority (von Knorring et al., 2010) and are entitled to influence such potent organizational components as structure, promotion paths and resource allocation.

Stoeckle (1988) claims that computer technology would permit to keep a close watch over physicians' decision-making. Technologies such as automated systems for detecting drug interactions or expert systems for medical diagnosis may serve as examples. One should also mention information systems (HIS), which are widely used in contemporary hospitals and collect large amounts of data about treatment processes, including physicians' activities, thereby providing extensive opportunity to perform detailed analyses of doctors' performance.

Dimensions of physicians' productivity

In ambulatory care, physicians' productivity is assessed by the number of clinical services, visits, and distinct patients per working day (e.g. Kantarevic et al., 2011). On the other hand, a more complex pattern of services as well as higher and more diverse costs make these simple productivity measures insufficient in hospitals, which should therefore be extended to additional dimensions.

Generally, productivity can be defined as the ratio of output to input usage (cf. Hollingsworth, 2008). Similarly, hospital productivity can be measured as the ratio of output (discharged patients) to input (labor, materials, energy, etc.). Since the reimbursement rates in case-mix systems are related to the number of discharged patients, their condition, comorbidities, as well as the applied treatment, the output can be measured by hospital revenue. Correspondingly, input may be measured by costs incurred for patient care. Therefore, the productivity of physicians from the hospital (managerial) perspective can be measured as the number of medical procedures performed by clinicians per unit of time or by the revenue which they generate from reimbursement in relation to the costs of treatment. Due to the volume of the article, other inputs influencing physicians' productivity such as support staff, medical equipment, office space, as well as other elements like the society, individual patients, and the third-party purchaser, will be omitted in further analysis.

In a case-mix system, the reimbursement rate should be determined by a patient's complexity. Thus, in the perfect reimbursement system that would include all costs on an adequate level for a specific hospital (the cost of a particular medical procedure can vary across hospitals), revenue would depend largely on physicians' productivity. However, perfect systems do not exist, thus the treatment of some diseases at certain hospitals will achieve a higher financial surplus (reimbursement rate compared to costs) than in others, which exerts pressure to treat more patients that bring higher margin (cf. Björkgren et al., 2004; Kaplan and Haas, 2014). Since the reimbursement system is far from perfect and there are differences in the costs of delivery across health services, this has far-reaching consequences for hospital management. Hospitals can improve their financial situation not only by means of cutting costs and increasing physicians' productivity related to the number of provided services, but also through the selection of patients and by initiating clinical activities that influence the reimbursement rates. For example, hospitals use specialist software to identify diagnostic codes and associated features such as length of stay (LOS) and medical procedures, which allows to plan medical processes in a way that will maximize case-mix tariffs and consequently, the hospital's revenue (cf. Covaleski et al., 1993; Samuel et al., 2005; Moryś, 2012).

Lewandowski (2014) identified four generic areas of control that allow managers to influence hospital input and output: (1) revenue control regarding the number of admitted patients and optimal case-mix coding determining the level of reimbursement; (2) control of the legitimacy of applied treatment in relation to the patient's condition; (3) input control (e.g. appropriate selection of patients in the emergency room); (4) control of the overall hospital costs, including, among others, the cost of drugs (e.g. generics), disposable materials, facility utilization, and staff remuneration. However, most of these areas are under physicians' jurisdiction and depend on their behavior.

Harrison and Ahmad (2000) claim that physicians' autonomy in everyday practice involves discretion and control over four major areas:

1) Diagnosis and treatment – decisions concerning the selection of methods for diagnosis and treatment, whom to refer and where, which drugs and procedures are to be used.
2) Evaluations of care – judgments concerning the correctness of care applied to a particular patient or the overall patterns of provided care.
3) Nature and volume of medical tasks – the ability of doctors to avoid being managed: to which extent doctors are left to determine their own timing, priorities, and workloads.
4) Contractual independence – refers directly to the characteristics of doctors' contracts of employment: to which extent clinicians have autonomous rights to engage in extracurricular activities such as research, teaching, scientific associations, private practice, especially within working hours.

In the light of the above definition of productivity, all fields of physicians' autonomy identified by Harrison and Ahmad (2000) relate to productivity. The first two areas refer to both patients' conditions and comorbidities, which determine the time and skills needed to diagnose and cure, as well as the level of costs of treatment and reimbursement rates associated with patients. The last two areas concern directly the time which physicians spend on treatment instead of performing other activities, thereby not contributing to hospital revenue.

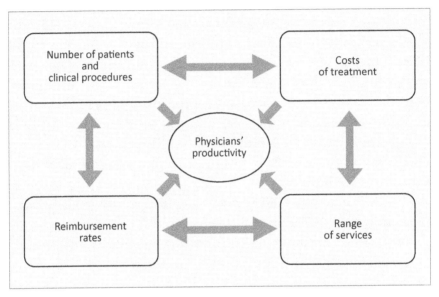

Figure 1. Dimensions of physicians' productivity

Source: prepared by the author.

Thus, taking into account the areas of autonomy and control, physicians' productivity can be measured in four dimensions: (1) the number of treated patients and provided clinical procedures; (2) range of services; (3) costs of treatment, and (4) reimbursement rates. The former merely describes the number of patients or procedures directly performed by a doctor; it may also be adjusted for patients' complexity. This dimension is related directly to the time which a physician will spend on patients' treatment. The second dimension is determined by the type of patients (diseases treated, with or without certain comorbidities). For example, one physician may be treating patients with a certain disease, but if a patient suffers from certain comorbidities like hypertension, he will send him or her to another provider. The third and fourth dimensions in an ideal reimbursement system can be immediate and direct consequences of the first two. However, in real healthcare systems, these dimensions are to some extent autonomous and depend on the decisions of physicians. In case-mix systems, the reimbursement rate will depend not only on patient conditions and comorbidities but also a number of factors related to the treatment process (e.g., LOS, type of applied diagnostics, and treatment). When planning the treatment process, physicians can impact the costs as well as the reimbursement rates, and consequently hospitals' revenue and financial results.

Of course, physicians' productivity also depends on their knowledge and skills in diagnosing and curing patients. More knowledgeable clinicians can diagnose and treat patients faster and with fewer resources, saving time and other costs. Similarly, skillful doctors may perform more sophisticated procedures, for example, one orthopedist can manage only small arthroscopies, while the other will perform complex spine surgeries. Nevertheless, this article does not concern physicians' capabilities – it discusses managerial control over the clinical productivity of individual physicians and the autonomy of doctors in the context of hospitals' financial sustainability. Therefore, the remaining portion of the paper shall omit issues concerning physicians' training and its influence on productivity unless they relate to autonomy or control.

Methods

For the purpose of this qualitative study, we have identified hospitals with a large pending scientific project concerning managerial control in public hospitals. The managers of three hospitals who claim to have experience in the introduction of quantitative measurement systems for the clinical activity of individual physicians were invited to enroll. The analysis comprises 2 multidisciplinary provincial hospitals (called PH1 and PH2) with 600 and 480 beds, 1000 and 750 employees, and 19 and 15 hospital wards, respectively, as well as and 1 district hospital with 9 medical wards, 256 beds and 420 employees (further called DH). All hospitals are public, financed according to case-mix, fee-for-service systems, and located in different parts of Poland. The distances that separate them make cooperation impossible. The financial situation in these hospitals is not critical, but they struggle to balance their costs by revenue.

Interviews were conducted with the hospitals' general managers (3 participants), medical directors (3 participants), heads of the wards (7 participants) and physicians (8 participants). In total, we conducted 21 semi-structured interviews during personal meetings. There were also a few phone re-interviews performed to supplement and clarify previously gathered information. All interviews were recorded by means of digital equipment, and then transcribed and analyzed. In this paper, the general directors of the hospitals and their deputies shall be regarded as managers, while the heads of wards, even though they partly play a managerial role, are classified as clinicians. The duration of interviews ranged from 30 to 90 minutes and began with open questions concerning the reasons and methods of control of hospital productivity. Further questions concerned the specific features of control of individual physicians' clinical practice. For example: How did you select quantitative measures? Did the physicians participate in the implementation process? What were the clinicians' reactions to detailed individual productivity reports? The questions were suited to the managers and the physicians. The research aimed to identify and understand the motives and methods employed by the managers to tighten control over physicians' productivity as well as the roots and modes of doctors' resistance.

The Polish context of reimbursement systems for in-patient services

In some cases, the reimbursement rates in Poland for patients treated within the case-mix system (JGP, or Jednorodne Grupy Pacjentów – the Polish version of DRG) are significantly inadequate for the average costs of their delivery. This means that certain medical specialties (departments) are effortlessly balancing the costs with revenues (such as interventional cardiology), while others are permanently in deficit (such as rehabilitation). There are also major differences inside specializations, for example within a range of procedures performed at traumatology and orthopedics departments, elective spine surgery or hip replacement have a greater likelihood of generating more profit than traumatology orthopedics. The profitability of a number of other specializations is not so evident – it depends on many variables, frequently unique to particular settings, including the pattern of delivered services, the economy of scale (variable and fixed costs ratio), and patient admission management (Lewandowski, 2014).

Additionally, Polish hospitals are able to increase their revenue mostly through delivering more services than was agreed with the payer at the beginning of the financial year (called collateral services further in the paper). According to the degressive payment scheme, there is no guarantee of full reimbursement, however, collateral services form the basis for expanding the contract in the subsequent year. Many medical departments can meet their costs only when delivering collateral services which will be reimbursed in a significant share of their contractual price. From a financial point of view, the best collateral services have a low ratio of variable costs, which means that payment of each additional service will recoup also a part of the hospital's fixed costs. The above reimbursement system demonstrates that control of delivered services might significantly improve the financial situation of the hospital.

Results

Physicians' productivity at the two studied hospitals was subject to frequent control in the form of remuneration executed through different legal relations, such as full-time employment based on the Code of Labor and civil law contracts. For example, in two hospitals (PH1 and PH2), the physicians in surgical wards were employed based on civil law contracts, and their income was related directly to the revenue generated by them. The revenue was calculated as stipulated in the contract percentage of 'earned' JGP points. In non-surgical departments, physicians were paid for the number of hours worked and their remuneration was not related to the ward's revenue. In two hospitals, all clinicians from non-surgical wards obtained the same rate per hour, while the physicians working at wards in the third hospital who achieved poorer financial results were remunerated lower than their colleagues from wards with a better financial situation. However, the system was frequently questioned. Physicians were raising the issue of inequality in terms of salaries; managers, on the other hand, indicated the lack of correlation between salary and workload. The problem was the most severe at the non-surgical wards where physicians' remuneration was not directly linked to the reimbursement rate from the national payer. Additionally, due to imperfection of the reimbursement system, the executives were not able to judge whether the negative economic result of a particular department originated from under-reimbursement or from doctors' low productivity. Managers claimed that the main obstacle in managing the hospital was a lack of reliable quantitative indicators of productivity for individual physicians. In their opinion, with such a system in place, certain physicians could deliver fewer services without compromising quality. The head of PH1 described this problem as follows:

> I have medical departments which meet costs even though their services are not well priced, but they perform more procedures and admit more patients per physician than the others [...] But I have also such [departments] which are deficient despite that their procedures are quite well paid. [...] They do not perform enough procedures to fulfill the contract, claiming that they have too much work, but in my opinion, it is not true.

During the interviews, managers also drew attention to conflicts over unequal workload between physicians. Some doctors often raised this issue in private conversations with managers, complaining that in some departments, physicians were working significantly less than in others. Sometimes, there are differences in workload even within the same ward. The medical director of DH quoted a conversation with the chief of the general surgery department:

> If the orthopedics [doctors from the department] thought a little, [...] trained themselves and entered into 'larger' more sophisticated procedures, [...] then they would meet costs [...] we also [doctors from general surgery department] could only accept 'easy' patients, and transfer the rest to other hospitals, then I wonder how our [financial] results would look like.

However, due to the lack of reliable data about the workload of individual physicians, the issue has seldom been raised officially. One physician said:

> When I once raised the problem [about unequal workload] the conversation ended with no conclusions since I had no reliable proof. [...] only some colleagues felt insulted.

Executives were aware that the physicians in some departments, who had greater responsibility for the hospital finances, work too hard, serve too many beds and keep costs too low. This compromises quality and might lead to medical errors. Managers were also aware that in the long run, these physicians might refuse to maintain this pattern and hospital sustainability would be threatened, therefore they have to equalize workload between physicians.

Managers expected that they could use the MSIPP to improve the hospital's financial sustainability. They thought that reliable and detailed data would allow to tighten control over physicians' day-to-day clinical practice and to enhance doctors' accountability for departmental and hospital financial results. Some managers believed that the MSIPP would be expected by those physicians who feel dissatisfied with the current division of labor, and they even planned to implement a motivational system that would allow to better align the objectives of clinicians working in non-surgical wards with financial priorities.

Implementation of the MSIPP

Managers were aware that a comparison of productivity between physicians practicing in different kinds of medical departments requires measures that would be accurate, objective, linked to the ward's clinical activities, and acceptable to medical professionals. Each surveyed hospital chose different methods to include the above requirements into the MSIPP. In PH1 and DH, the managers based the system on data from the hospital information system (HIS), while in PH2, due to the lack of comprehensive HIS, medical staff (later also some administrative personnel) was asked to assess the number of medical procedures performed by each physician using their own observations as well as a less sophisticated IT system, which is normally used for settlement of the medical services with the payer (NFZ).

Provincial hospital 1 (PH1)

In PH1, the management proposed to introduce special coefficients related to the time a physician needs to devote to a patient depending on their conditions and comorbidities. The idea behind this concept was to gain evidence that despite the fact that monthly revenue and the number of treated patients per doctor in the non-surgical wards are frequently lower than in the surgical ones, the workload may be comparable. For example, in the non-surgical wards such as rheumatology, endocrinology, or geriatrics, the doctors treated fewer patients per month because of their longer average hospitalization; physicians require more time to analyze the medical records of those patients. The physicians with these specialties often play the part of 'investigators' who have to establish the cause of symptoms in the long process of diagnostics and analysis based on the exclusion of some conditions, rather than on direct diagnosis.

In the beginning, the managers in PH1 prepared the preliminary coefficients as a starting point by themselves. They elaborated a report comparing the productivity of individual physicians, including the new coefficient on each ward, and prepared a presentation thereof. As the managers predicted, clinicians were skeptical about the coefficients as well as the idea of measurement and comparison. Thus, the managers proposed that the clinicians 'fix' the productivity measurement system. But, in one way or another, physicians answered that the comparison of doctors by numbers was impossible since everyone had their own specific work characteristics. In this situation, managers tried to engage in the project only those physicians who they thought would certainly gain from the introduction of the system (those which complained about inequality in workload). Surprisingly, these clinicians also refused to participate since they failed to see any need, benefits or possibility to measure individual clinical activities concerning their time schedule. According to the head of the rheumatology:

I don't want my doctors to work under pressure, that they have to treat more patients because our measures would be lower than in other wards. [...] They might make a medical error.

On the other hand, physicians agreed to participate in cost containing and revenue (reimbursement rates) optimization initiatives and accepted managerial suggestions towards the selection of patients admitted to the hospital. An orthopedist said:

Previously we accepted all patients and called for external consultation when we had a problem. Now, we are referring them to the hospital which has greater experience with that medical problem. [...] It really saves a lot of time and costs. [...] We can concentrate on patients whom we know how to cure.

Provincial hospital 2 (PH2)

In the PH2, the HIS was not fully developed, therefore, it was difficult to obtain trustworthy data concerning the clinical activity of individual physicians. Managers proposed that physicians should register their activity by themselves to build reliable track records. However, the heads of wards and senior consultants tried to find an excuse in the form of the lack of time for such work. To help them, the medical director organized a team of young volunteer physicians who were asked to register the number of delivered services by each physician and measure the time needed for certain stages of patient treatment (medical record analysis, patient examination, treatment planning, etc.). After a few weeks, young doctors started to withdraw from the team. In private conversations they admitted that their older colleagues questioned their results, claiming that they were not experienced enough to prepare such records. They were advised not to participate in this activity.

Managers undertook another round of discussion with the senior clinicians. Because they were prepared that physicians would use their customary 'quality and safety' arguments, the managers attempted to promise a financial reward for developing a productivity measurement system and to convince physicians that its sole goal would be to reduce conflicts between physicians and to raise the salaries for better performers, while there would be no reduction for others. Consequently, if the project was to be successful and lead to increase productivity, the salaries could rise for all. However, this proposal was not well received. Doctors claimed that the intensity of physicians' work could not be described and measured easily. They also mentioned that non-clinicians were unable to understand the specifics of medical work, and therefore the measures might be used wrongly. In the light of this fact, they refused to cooperate. The medical director of PH2 described the situation as follows:

> The fact that those, [doctors] who are less burdened with work would protest, it was obvious. [...] But I was surprised that even those of my colleagues who have for years complained about their hard work, and claimed that others have time for 'coffee and gossip' also did not want to cooperate.

Physicians, however, do not object to discussing the costs and reimbursement rates generated by them. Furthermore, they advised the managers on which patients they were prepared to treat with high cost-effectiveness and what were the reasonable scopes of amendments of a treatment plan in order to obtain better reimbursement rates without harming patients.

District hospital (DH)

The DH director decided to introduce measurement of doctors' productivity by means of the HIS data which contains patient records and all related clinical activities. Based on the HIS, all medical consultations and procedures, as well as the revenue and costs generated by patients treated by individual doctors, were calculated. When the director first presented the quantitative data for each physician, she took note of a great deal of consternation among the doctors, who were surprised that such information could be so easily obtained from the HIS. But no physician in this hospital was content with the measurement as well, regardless of whether they were the leader in terms of the numbers or not. A discussion was opened regarding the costs and reimbursement rates that could be obtained depending on the method of patient treatment, LOS and appropriate coding in JGP groups, but they refused even to debate about their activities concerning the time spent on patient care or a comparison of the number of discharges per physician.

Generally, quantitative data regarding physicians' clinical activity was very reluctantly received and questioned as not reflecting the real workload. Also, doctors did not accept the statistical analysis of their clinical work. Nevertheless, the director of the DH was strongly determined to implement the MSIPP as a base for the bonus system. She attempted to build a team with a view to developing adequate measures, but there were no doctors willing to participate. The director started to offer additional remuneration for work in the team, but it sent the wrong message and was understood as a kind of bribery, which aggravated the atmosphere around the idea of measurement. During the interview, the DH medical director complained:

> When I was pressing them [doctors] harder, by proposing money, the heads of wards started to demand better equipment and access to a wider range of tests in the hospital laboratory [...] or were complaining that there are too few nurses in their wards, [...] that patient safety is compromised. Generally, they were trying to find the weak spots in the hospital and attack there. [...] They simply wanted to show me that there were so many needs to be financed, that spending money on the measurement system was a stupidity.

The general director did not hide her disappointment:

> Their attitude [senior doctors] really hinders health care efficiency. In many wards, physicians working really hard, they exceed the contract [with NFZ], but on others, [...], I am convinced that they can do more.

The interviewed physicians indicated that they were not against reasonable cost reduction, budgeting, performance measurement on the department level, but they were strongly against the MSIPP. One physician said:

> Sometimes there is a patient, that I couldn't find the cause for his symptoms for many days, but with others, I need ten minutes to diagnose [...] how to measure my productivity? Medicine it is not a production line!

Surprisingly, clinicians accepted reimbursement optimization when it related to minor amendments of the treatment plan, and to the scope of delivered services. According to the words of an internal medicine physician:

> If extending patients' LOS just for one or two days or adding some diagnostics would improve our reimbursement rate, I am not against it. We also can control to some extent the pattern of patients we admit to our ward but control of our time schedules is unacceptable.

Another doctor further explained it in more detail:

> Managers think that I should take care of everybody from my specialty and refer no patients to other hospitals, especially those who are well priced, but sometimes I feel that I can't treat [...] just this patient. I'm afraid that I cannot handle that [...] I will make a mistake and I will be in trouble. There would be a risk for patients and for me.

In summary, the managers in all hospitals did not abandon the publication of productivity reports concerning the clinical activities of individual physicians, although in a restrained scope and without doctors' involvement and their official acceptance. Thus, managers were not able to use data from MSIPP as a basis for remuneration systems or formal comparison of physicians' workloads. Surprisingly, it appears that the reports regarding physicians' workload have been occasionally exploited by physicians themselves, especially in the discussions between departments and even with managers – when the data supported the doctor's point of view. Some managers admitted that they did not have solid proof, however, they felt that the discussions concerning physicians' time schedule had been more productive and less emotional even though the reports were not officially referred to.

Discussion

The research showed that managers have been trying to control the productivity of individual physicians in all four dimensions (Figure 1) and to some extent, doctors have accepted the productivity measures related to cost of treatment, reimbursement rates, and the range of services but have strongly opposed to measurement of the number of patients and clinical procedures performed by them when it concerns the time which they spend on patient care. Managers were unable to engage physicians in the development of quantitative measures allowing objective assessment of their time schedule, even though executives attempted to exploit the conflict between physicians and involve the clinicians who have complained about unequal workload. It appeared that the defense of this area of professional autonomy was more important than workload inequality, and even than individual financial benefits. Whatever managers were trying to present as their intentions, clinicians were suspicious that the measurement could be used not only to equalize the workload but also to extend managerial control over physicians' clinical activities – especially over their time schedule. The official reasons for the physicians' refusal were that: the MSIPP is unnecessary because they already do their best; there are better goals for spending money; pressure to increase productivity might compromise quality and safety of care; and finally, that clinical activity could not be measured since it is too complex.

However, the research revealed that measurement systems, even those not officially accepted by physicians, have allowed managerial encroachment into clinical practice and to some extent affect all areas of physicians' autonomy described by Harrison and Ahmad (2000). Managers were able to exert pressure and influence physicians' decisions concerning patient selection and treatment in such a way that would allow to increase the hospital revenue. To a lesser extent, managers were able to undermine clinicians' autonomy referring to the volume of their medical tasks (workloads and timing) and consequently, the degree to which doctors could engage in extracurricular activities, also outside the hospital, in their working time.

There was also another factor mentioned in the interviews which could have potentially increased resistance – risk aversion. Some physicians, despite being aware that their profession was associated with risk, have tried to minimize it by referring patients to other wards or hospitals, in spite of having formal qualifications and training to treat those patients.

The source of resistance to managerial control may also be rooted deeper in the structure of the profession and their jurisdiction, since every move in one profession jurisdiction affects those of others (Abbott, 1988), so managerial encroachment into clinical practice impacts the jurisdiction of doctors. With the proposed measurement system, managers can take control over part of professional knowledge, making it less abstract and more available through its quantification. As Abbott (1988) claimed, the abstraction of professional work enables survival and power. Control will not affect their knowledge but will influence the way in which it is executed and how it can be used for one's own benefits.

Control practices are based on power relations and often evoke resistance, but not many employees are able to avoid it. This research shows that physicians largely have been capable of defending their autonomy against managerial encroachment into their time schedule and workload. Such resistance might be effective due to the complex nature of medical practice, which is often based on teamwork and rooted in clinical expertise. The development of control methods concerning clinical activity is to some extent feasible without the involvement of physicians, however, introducing physicians in the organization as an official standard is practically impossible since the 'production process' depends on clinical expertise. Medical profession controls not only the process of clinical work but also its assessment (Barley and Tolbert, 1991; Derber and Schwartz, 1991). Physicians are experts who produce scientific evidence and medical guidelines on which standards are based (Kuhlmann and Burau, 2008). Also, the strong position of physicians in the labor market has allowed them to openly deny participation in the measurement system. Clan-based control mechanisms (cf. Ouchi, 1979) that function inside the medical profession support senior clinicians in influencing their younger colleagues and discouraging them from participating in managerial initiatives. Even internal conflicts inside medical profession seemed insufficiently strong to break the collective defense of clinical autonomy.

The main power in managerial disposition, i.e., resource allocation, also appears incapable of breaking doctors' resistance relating to the control of their time schedule. Firstly, the proposition of direct payment for participation in the implementation was obviously in contradiction with the professional ideology that grants priority to perform socially valuable and needed work over economic profitability and self-rewards (Freidson, 2001). It could not be treated differently than an attempt of bribery. Secondly, the managerial power of resource allocation is to some extent elusive as doctors are individuals who decide about standards of care, and consequently about the consumption of resources.

It has been an interesting observation that physicians were opposed to the implementation of quantitative measurement of their individual clinical activity by executives, but started to use quantitative data from managerial reports for their own purposes. While deciding to combat the managerial system on the one hand, they later colonized it and adopted the idea into their professional self-regulation processes, preventing the managers from interfering.

Conclusion

The research allows to deepen the understanding of the motives and methods that managers have attempted to employ to tighten control over physicians' productivity as well as the roots and modes of doctors' resistance. It appears that executives have been unable to equally restrain professional autonomy in the four areas mentioned by Harrison and Ahmad (2000). Doctors are particularly strongly opposed to the measurement of their workload. On the other hand, managers were able to use the MSIPP to increase the pressure exerted on physicians and to influence their productivity concerning the cost of treatment, reimbursement rates, and the range of services (Figure 1). But, despite their formal position in the hospital hierarchy and access to medical records, they were unable to control physicians' productivity regarding the number of patients and clinical procedures. Nevertheless, managers reported that the publication of data about physicians' workloads, even without their involvement and approval, has brought positive effects, since doctors have informally adopted some quantitative measures into their self-governing processes.

Managerial endeavors to tighten control over clinical processes and physicians' resistance should be also considered from the standpoint of social welfare. The intention of governments to employ managers in hospitals was to lower the overall inpatients' costs. However, managers who are responsible for the organization, rather than healthcare systems, use all methods at their hands to ensure hospitals' sustainability. The most controversial measures include patient selection and the increase of remuneration rates. The former might be positive if it succeeds in preventing the 'fragmentation of population such that most providers have not a critical mass of patients with a given medical condition' (Porter and Lee, 2013, p. 53) since it increases experience, quality, and likely cost-effectiveness. The latter may be justified if it serves as the only way to prevent under-reimbursement and keeps the hospital functioning at a level that allows providing patients with safe and optimal quality services (cf. Smith, 2002; Porter and Lee, 2013).

The autonomy of physicians, on the other hand, should restrain managerial pressure to that extent which would protect patients from risks and low quality resulting from, for example, lack of clinicians' training. In this context, it could be argued whether extracurricular activities are only in the interests of the society since they consist of additional training and scientific work or are overused to achieve the individual interests of physicians such as additional income. In the light of this fact, this situation should remain under managerial control to prevent deterioration of the hospital's efficiency. Hence, in lies in the interest of for social welfare to seek optimal equilibrium between professional autonomy and managerial control in order to build a self-regulating system based on opposing, albeit complementary forces.

From a practical point of view, the research shows that implementing a "productivity measurement of individual physicians is not a panacea for better control over hospitals' costs and revenue. However, publications of detailed data concerning physicians' clinical activity, even not supported by physicians, may serve as the best alternative at the disposal of managers for exercising any influence (though indirect) over physicians' productivity.

The main limitation of the study is the sample selection and the sincerity of received interviews. The described hospitals were chosen from a limited group, and it is not known whether there exist other settings where managers have attempted to implement some kind of measurement system of individual physicians' productivity, and if they have achieved other outcomes. Secondly, the questions asked relate, to some extent, to controversial issues, thus the interviewees may have hidden certain information even though they were assured about their anonymity.

References

Abbott A. (1988). *The System of Professions: An Essay on the Division of Labor.* Chicago: University of Chicago Press.

Abernethy M.A., Brownell P. and Clegg S. (2006). "Accounting and control in health care: Behavioural, organisational, sociological and critical perspectives". In: *Handbooks of Management Accounting Research*, C.S. Chapman, A.G. Hopwood and M.D. Shields (eds.) (Vol. 2, 805–829). New York: Elsevier.

Barley S. R. and Tolbert P. S. (1991). "Introduction: At the intersection of organizations and occupations". *Research in Sociology of Organizations* 9, 1–16.

Birch S., Kephart G., Tomblin Murphy G., O'Brien-Pallas L. and Alder R. (2009). "Health human resources planning and the production of health: Development of an extended analytical framework for needs-based health human resources planning". *Journal of Public Health Management and Practice* 15 (Suppl), S56–S61.

Björkgren M., Hjalte F., Molin R. and Gerdtham U.G. (2004). "Case-mix adjustment and efficiency measurement". *Scandinavian Journal of Public Health* 32(6), 464–471. https://doi.org/10.1080/14034940410028235.

Checkland K., McDonald R., Harrison S. and Grant S. (2007). "Ticking boxes and changing the social world: Data collection and the New UK General Practice Contract". *Social Policy & Administration* 41(7), 693–710.

Chilingerian J.A. and Sherman H.D. (1990). "Managing physician efficiency and effectiveness in providing hospital services". *Health Services Management Research* 3(1), 3–15.

Covaleski M.A., Dirsmith M.W. and Michelman J.E. (1993). "An institutional theory perspective on the DRG framework, case-mix accounting systems and healthcare organizations". *Accounting, Organizations and Society* 18(1), 65–80.

Derber C. and Schwartz W.A. (1991). "New mandarins or new proletariat? Professional power at work". *Research in the Sociology of Organizations* 8(1), 71–96.

Doolin B. (1999). "Casemix management in a New Zealand hospital: Rationalisation and resistance". *Financial Accountability and Management* 15(3–4), 397–417. https://doi.org/10.1111/1468-0408.00033.

Eurostat Statistics Explained (2016). *Healthcare expenditure by provider, 2012 (% of current health expenditure).* http://ec.europa.eu/eurostat/statistics-explained/index.php/Healthcare_statistics..

Freidson E. (1986). *Professional Powers: A Study of the Institutionalization of Formal Knowledge*. Chicago: University of Chicago Press.

Freidson E. (1988). *Profession of Medicine: A Study of the Sociology of Applied Knowledge*. Chicago: University of Chicago Press.

Freidson E. (2001). *Professionalism, the Third Logic: On the Practice of Knowledge*. Chicago: University of Chicago Press.

Goes J.B. and Zhan C. (1995). "The effects of hospital-physician integration strategies on hospital financial performance". *Health Services Research* 30(4), 507–530.

Harrison S. and Ahmad W.I.U. (2000). "Medical autonomy and the UK state 1975 to 2025". *Sociology* 34(1), 129–146.

Hollingsworth B. (2008). "The measurement of efficiency and productivity of health care delivery". *Health Economics* 17(10), 1107–1128. https://doi.org/10.1002/hec.1391.

Kantarevic J., Kralj B. and Weinkauf D. (2011). "Enhanced fee-for-service model and physician productivity: Evidence from family health groups in Ontario". *Journal of Health Economics* 30(1), 99–111. https://doi.org/10.1016/j.jhealeco.2010.11.006.

Kaplan R.S. and Haas D.A. (2014). "How not to cut health care costs". *Harvard Business Review* 92(11), 116–122.

Kaye A.D., Cornett E.M., Chalifoux A.L., Pittet J.F. and Hakim T.S. (2014). "Clinical performance feedback and quality improvement opportunities for perioperative physicians". *Advances in Medical Education and Practice*, 5, 115.

Kuhlmann E. and Burau V. (2008). "The 'healthcare state' in transition: National and international contexts of changing professional governance". *European Societies* 10(4), 619–633.

Kuhlmann E., Burau V., Correia T. et al. (2013). "'A manager in the minds of doctors': A comparison of new modes of control in European hospitals". *BMC Health Services Research* 13(1), 1.

Kuhlmann E., Burau V., Larsen C. et al. (2011). "Medicine and management in European healthcare systems: How do they matter in the control of clinical practice?". *International Journal of Clinical Practice* 65 (7), 722.

Lewandowski R.A. (2014). "Cost control of medical care in public hospitals – a comparative analysis". *International Journal of Contemporary Management* 13(1), 125–136.

Lewandowski R., Miszczyńska K., Antczak E. and Moryś J. (2020). "Ideology, trust, and spirituality: A framework for management control research in Industry 4.0

era". In: *The Future of Management. Industry 4.0 and Digitalization*, P. Buła and B. Nogalski (eds.) (72–91). Kraków: Jagiellonian University Press.

McDonald R., Harrison S., Checkland K. and Campbell S.M. (2007). "Impact of financial incentives on clinical autonomy and internal motivation in primary care: Ethnographic study". *British Medical Journal* 334(7608), 1357.

Miszczyńska K. and Antczak E. (2020). *Uwarunkowania zadłużenia szpitali w Polsce.* Łódź: Wydawnictwo Uniwersytetu Łódzkiego.

Moryś J. (2012). *List otwarty rektora Gdańskiego Uniwersytetu Medycznego do Przewodniczącego Rady Pomorskiego Oddziału Narodowego Funduszu Zdrowia.* Rynek Zdrowia – portal.

Noordegraaf M. (2011). "Risky business: How professionals and professional fields (must) deal with organizational issues". *Organization Studies* 32(10), 1349–1371. https://doi.org/10.1177/0170840611410832.

Noordegraaf M. (2020). "Protective or connective professionalism? How connected professionals can (still) act as autonomous and authoritative experts". *Journal of Professions and Organization* 7(2), 205–223.

Noordegraaf M. and Abma, T. (2003). "Management by measurement? Public management practices amidst ambiguity". *Public Administration* 81(4), 853–871. https://doi.org/10.1111/1467-9299.00370.

Ouchi W.G. (1979). "A conceptual framework for the design of organizational control mechanisms". *Management Science* 25(9), 833–848. https://doi.org/10.1287/mnsc.25.9.833.

Overeem K. (2011). "Doctor performance assessment: Development and impact of a new system" (Doctoral dissertation). https://doi.org/10.1007/s40037-012-0009-0.

Porter M.E. and Lee T. (2013). "Providers must lead the way in making value the overarching goal". *Harvard Business Review* 91(10), 50–70. https://hbr.org/2013/10/providers-must-lead-the-way-in-making-value-the-overarching-goal. Accessed: 28.11.2021.

Ramsey P.G. et al. (1993). "Use of peer ratings to evaluate physician performance". *Jama* 269(13), 1655–1660. https://doi.org/10.1001/jama.1993.03500130081035.

Rüsch S. (2016). "Cooperation between managers and the medical profession in the context of strategic decision-making in non-profit hospitals". In: *Ethics and Professionalism in Healthcare: Transition and Challenges*, S. Salloch, G. Sandow and M. Schildmann (eds.) (138–147). Abingdon on Thames: Routledge. https://www.taylorfrancis.com/books/e/9781315527466/chapters/10.4324/9781315527466-14. Accessed: 13.12.2021.

Samuel S. et al. (2005). "Monetized medicine: From the physical to the fiscal". *Accounting, Organizations and Society* 30(3), 249–278. https://doi.org/10.1016/j.aos.2004.02.001.

Smith P.C. (2002). "Measuring health system performance". *The European Journal of Health Economics* 3(3), 145–148. https://doi.org/10.1007/s10198-002-0138-1.

Stoeckle J.D. (1988). "Reflections on modern doctoring: [Introduction]". *The Milbank Quarterly*, 66, 76–91. https://doi.org/10.2307/3350101.

Van Der Vleuten C.P.M. (1996). "The assessment of professional competence: Developments, research and practical implications". *Advances in Health Sciences Education* 1(1), 41–67. https://doi.org/10.1007/BF00596229.

von Knorring M. et al. (2010). "Managers' perceptions of the manager role in relation to physicians: A qualitative interview study of the top managers in Swedish healthcare". *BMC Health Services Research* 10(1), 1. https://doi.org/10.1186/1472-6963-10-271.

VanHeuvelen J.S. (2020). "Professional engagement in articulation work: Implications for experiences of clinical and workplace autonomy". In: *Research in the Sociology of Work*, E.H. Gorman and S.P. Vallas (eds.) (11–31). Bingley: Emerald Publishing Limited.

ALEKSANDER NOWORÓL, D.Sc., Ph.D.
Krakow University of Economics

Hybridization of territorial development management

Abstract

The paper reveals the nature and forms of hybrid phenomena perceived in managing territorial development. The author's reflection observes hybrid phenomena in governance and spatial management to indicate hybridization as a specific operation pattern in the increasing complexity of territorial events. The essence of hybridization of development management represents an agile shift from hierarchical, vertically organized governance and management systems towards solutions distributed in the network and horizontal governance ecosystems. It means building social and managerial relations on a contractual basis in place of hierarchical dominion and coercion but also the dissemination of practices such as multi-level management, multi-sector partnerships, crowdsourcing, and crowdfunding.

Keywords: hybridization, territorial development management, governance, spatial management, network governance, multi-sector partnerships

Introduction

The paper reveals the nature and forms of hybrid phenomena identified in managing territorial development. The author's reflection observes hybrid phenomena in governance and public management to indicate hybridization as a specific operation pattern in the increasing complexity of territorial phenomena. This attempt aims to create a model in the form of a set of fundamental instruments that could serve as recommendations for the creators of the future of territorial units.

The essence of hybridization of governance and spatial management

A review of the scientific literature related to various forms of hybridization in governance and spatial management reveals fragmentary treatment of this problem. It is worth mentioning selected publications. Governance or management hybridization is most often described in the context of mixed organizational structures and their reciprocal impacts (Johanson and Vakkuri, 2018; Andersen and Sand, 2012). One example is large state-private companies that exert state control over economic life in countries such as Russia and Kazakhstan (Khana, 2012). In general, many publications refer to public-private partnerships in the provision of public services (Czarniawska and Solli, 2016; German and Keeler, 2010; Johanson and Vakkuri, 2018; Logvinov and Lebid, 2018), as well as their impact on public affairs management. Also essential are considerations regarding territorial cooperation in triple, quadruple, and quintuple helix models (Etzkowitz and Leydesdorff, 2000; Miron and Gherasim, 2018; Carayannis et al., 2012). Many publications deal with the hybridization of socio-economic development as a dimension that represents the complexity of contemporary development processes (Boyer, 1997; Drobniak, 2019; Rifkin, 2016), while other books and papers refer indirectly to development management, describing hybrid geography (Graham, 2008) or the complexity of spatial structures, including the non-adjustment of historical schemes to contemporary socio-economic and ideological realities (Golubchikov, 2016; Palej, 2010; Venturi, 1966). Yet another, also fragmentary, understanding of hybridization is associated with multiculturalism resulting from globalization (Pierterse, 2001; Wang and Yueh-yu Yeh, 2005). Perhaps the closest to the author's view are broad considerations regarding global shifts in management under the influence of technological changes (Anheier and Krlev, 2014; Elsner 2004).

A brief review that provides merely a partial reflection of the scale of the use of the concepts of hybrid or hybridization in the scientific literature leads to the following conclusions regarding the hybridization of management. Hybridization can take various forms, such as:

- combining various elements into a new, relatively coherent whole, usually constituting a new quality solution:
  - ◇ these elements may be spatial or related to human behavior and institutions more broadly, and correlate to new organizational systems: social, cultural, economic, management,
  - ◇ these elements can interact and lead to a blurring of boundaries,
- application and pressure to adopt specific solutions in the areas of programming, organization, and implementation in new contexts: spatial-geographical, socio-cultural, and organizational management,
- combining top-down and bottom-up approaches in multi-level and multi-stakeholder management processes,
- acting in a state of contradiction between the values or narratives of specific institutions and legal and organizational solutions related to economic restructuring or political change.

Subsequent processes related to the hybridization of management are related to the influence of the information society. Information and communication technologies (ICT) affect how public policies are conducted, including territorial development policies. In consequence, we observe the empowerment of communities that can have a direct impact on public affairs. Thus, it is revealed as an elimination of intermediaries in economic and social processes (called disintermediation). New technologies reduce the importance of the spatial factor in socio-economic relations, shortening the relative distances by facilitating communication (called despatialization). Both these factors support decentralization, shifting the paradigm of governance and influencing development policy. All three processes disturb the functioning of traditional forms of territorial development management. The related managerial means characterized by unprecedented complexity, and even by contradictions, can be called hybrid. This phenomenon seems to characterize such currently observed processes as multi-level governance, public-private public-social partnerships, crowdsourcing, as well as crowdfunding.

Hybridization as a process in governance and spatial management

Scientific elaborations have shed some light on the embedding of hybridization in contemporary theoretical concepts.

Ideas such as "network" and "partnership" are of key significance here. Already at the end of the 20th century, R.A.W. Rhodes noted the importance of self-organizing inter-organizational networks, pointing to their four characteristics: 1) inter-organization interdependence, which means including entities from outside the public sector and breaking the "boundaries" between the public, private and social spheres; 2) constant interactions between network participants caused by the need to exchange resources and negotiate goals; 3) game-like interactions, based on trust and regulated by rules, negotiated and agreed by network participants; as a consequence 4) a significant level of independence from the state, resulting from the fact that the networks are not accountable to the state; the state does not take a sovereign position over the network, but it can indirectly control them (Rhodes, 1997, p. 53).

I. Elander emphasizes the importance of cross-sector partnerships in creating public policies, and raises the following arguments:

- partnership can create synergistic effects for its participants,
- partnership spreads the risks of the project implementation among many actors,
- partnership can help one of the partners so that he can influence the world view and the way of action of other participants,
- partnership may serve as an instrument for obtaining additional funds for other participants,
- partnership can be a means of reducing open conflict and creating an atmosphere of compromise,
- partnership can reduce exorbitant demands on (self) government and create a broader, more fragmented basis for delivering tasks (Elander, 2002, p. 198).

Space management at various scales is often hybrid, therefore one can identify complex and mixed forms of space usage. The following examples can be evoked:

- transformations of historical building structures due to the adoption of new types and forms of use,
- transforming the urban tissue through new juxtapositions and collisions of models from different eras and design concepts,
- ideological conflicts – collisions of new ownership structures with the existing spatial structure,
- symbolic collisions related to suburbanization and the spatial chaos of the suburbs,
- hybridization of images and meanings imposed from ubiquitous advertisements (Noworól, 2020, p. 20).

In addition to the provided examples and presented aspects of hybridization, it is worth exploring an important feature in the form of combining contradictions. R. Venturi noticed that the contradictions in shaping space can assume two main features, i.e., they can be mutually adapted or collided (juxtaposed). The figure below interprets Venturi's concept and presents the essence of combining contradictions in a new creation with hybrid features.

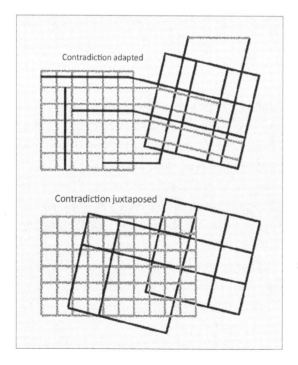

Figure 1. Contradictions, adapted and juxtaposed

Source: prepared by the author, inspired by: R. Venturi (1966). *Complexity and Contradiction in Architecture.* New York: The Museum of Modern Art.

The said forms of hybridization may overlap, but their essential feature will continue to be heterogeneity that leads to a high level of complexity.

Hybridization as a method of territorial change

It is worth recalling some concepts from spatial economy that draw from the elements of hybridization.

Territory is a phenomenon in which different types of elements remain in a constantly changing interdependence. The material and non-material aspects of territories are emphasized by the so-called **territorial capital**. Territorial capital concerns the relationship between territorial elements that are important for explaining the models of regional development (Camagni et al., 2011, p. 4). Territorial capital is defined as a set of localized (immobile) resources: natural, human, artificial (cultural), organizational and cognitive, which constitute the competitive potential of a territory (Camagni et al., 2011, p. 61). The conditions and facilities that create territorial capital provide effective mechanisms for developing and supporting the productivity and effectiveness of local enterprises. This capital consists of institutions, decision-making models, and social competencies. The elements of territorial capital are organized on a three-level scale according to two criteria: rivalry and materiality.

Club goods and impure public goods can be found on the axis of rivalry between public and private goods. As part of the second criterion, mixed goods fall between tangible goods (hard) and intangible goods (soft). An intermediate class of club goods and impure public goods requires a new approach to development management based on mixed ownership, territorial cooperation, and the ability to network and open up to social participation in programming and development (Camagni 2008, p. 38; Camagni et al., 2011, p. 5).

Soft planning spaces is another essential concept that combines the spatial and managerial dimensions (Allmendinger and Haughton, 2009). Soft planning spaces is described by Ł. Mikuła, who demonstrates the merge of management practices in changing institutional conditions within functional urban areas. Mikuła emphasizes that today, spatial reflection combines two determinants. On the one hand, it is about geographical determinants, i.e., overlapping territories in changing forms with undefined borders, while on the other, we are dealing with "institutionally soft" spaces. It is about not having the status of territorial division units – areas that are subject to territorial management but at the same time devoid of "a clear statutory basis and legal and institutional framework" (Mikuła, 2019, p. 42). Soft spaces are characterized by ambiguity, both in terms of spatial delimitation and anchoring in the legal and administrative system. The identification of soft spaces results from various types of flows of people, goods, services, capital, information, as well as self-organization of territorial communities and political decisions. In their nature, soft spaces are an example of a hybrid creation.

Organizational and institutional hybridization is at the foundation of H. Etzkowitz and L. Leydesdorff's classic model of creating knowledge – and an economy based on it – through the so-called **triple helix**. The model assumes close cooperation between universities, businesses, and administration, intertwining similar elements of the DNA helix. The authors believe that the triple helix generates an infrastructure of knowledge in terms of overlapping institutional spheres, each of which takes on the role of the other, resulting in the emergence of interfaces that take the form of hybrid organizations (Etzkowitz and Leydesdorff, 2000, p. 112). The concept of Etzkowitz and Leydesdorff has been developed as a fourfold *quadruple* helix (Miron and Gherasim, 2018) and a fivefold *quintuple* helix (Carayannis et al., 2012), which seems to be particularly fertile in inspiring the hybridization of management.

The most developed reflection in this regard is proposed by E.G. Carayannis, T.D. Barth, and D. Campbell, who describe a concept that integrates environmental issues into earlier models of intersectoral cooperation. The necessity of partnership cooperation is indicated here: science (universities), business, administration, media, and social organizations in the context of reflection on the quality of the natural environment as an element of production processes, and at the same time innovation. This context applies to entities that are holders and bodies controlling the state of environmental resources. Another critical aspect of environmental issues consists in influencing new lifestyles and consumption models, considering climatic issues, environmental cleanliness, knowledge, know-how, and sustainable development

(Carayannis et al., 2012). As a consequence, a five-step sequence of activity can be outlined:

- universities developing scientific research and providing educational services, resulting in innovative solutions and increasing human capital while serving as a leaven of innovative economic concepts,
- business that creates values in the sphere of knowledge-based economy, conditioning the emergence of new professions, products, and services through environmentally friendly technologies (e.g., using recycling elements),
- entities related to the disposal and control of environmental resources in a manner limiting its exploitation, the formation of pollution and waste of these resources, and at the same time helping to redefine quality of life in balance with nature,
- media and society, making people aware of how and to what extent a higher quality of life influences communication, and consequently creating new models of community functioning, modifying lifestyles while taking into account environmental aspects,
- administration and political system that perform in the context of new needs and changing levels of citizens' satisfaction. At the same time, there is a rise of new expectations from the political system and public administration, which should generate impulses for educational activities, lead to the development of a knowledge-based economy, and ensure democratic order and environmental standards.

Hybridization model

The territorial development management of today has assumed a dual nature. On the one hand, it has always comprised an attempt to organize material reality concerning the – inherently abstract – game of social forces, taking the form of leading institutions and the will of leaders under the conditions of a certain level of technological development. However, on the other hand, new conditions related to the flourishing of information and communication technologies disrupt traditional connections, creating new liaisons, and thus – a paradigm in which the notions of "network" and "clouds" collide with traditional social hierarchies, their power, and economic domination.

For contemporary development management, this means a dynamic transition between opposites in the context of the constantly changing conditions for decision-making. The essence of hybridization in the context of development management represents an agile – and often partially or/and temporarily reversible – shift from hierarchical, vertically organized governance and management systems to solutions distributed in the network and horizontal governance ecosystems. It means building social and managerial relations on the contractual model in place of hierarchical dominion and coercion. Thus, the hybrid co-management process involves making the following, sometimes multiple, changes:

- from exclusivity and domination of elite influence to inclusive social participation, with all the wealth of attitudes and at the same time – different levels of competence and understanding of the consequences of decisions made,
- from the dominion concentrated in the central center of power to dominion of the community, guided by the often divergent and difficult to coordinate individual and group interests,
- from concentrating development management processes within administrative units to coordinating the impact on the ecosystem of public, economic, and social entities that operate in the scale of soft spaces and functional areas,
- from the formulation of development strategies by leaders and political parties to deliberative panels considering political forces, economic, social, and environmental organizations, as well as the voice of individual members of society used in the crowdsourcing process,
- from managing public entities responsible for territorial development to:
  ◇ controlling platforms of cooperating organizations that perform tasks in the outsourcing model, and even up to,
  ◇ institutional change and shaping social attitudes, allowing for orientation in the complexities of the contemporary world,
- from managing a specific public, economic or social entity to a distributed collaborative community,

- from centralized financing of development by a public or private entity to various configurations of partnership solutions in a complex financial assembly, including crowdfunding, i.e., distributed social financing,
- from educating a penal society focused on technocratic tasks in a uniform cultural model to education open to diversity, willingness to learn about otherness and building – based on soft competences – a harmonious community that understands the place of man in the face of climatic and environmental challenges,
- from monitoring and evaluation carried out by officials and experts to a broad understanding of the effects of planned interventions by territorial communities.

This transition between the two ways of understanding governance is well illustrated by the helix model, which reflects the counterpoint effect in shaping implementation instruments under the conditions of management hybridization (see Figure 2 below).

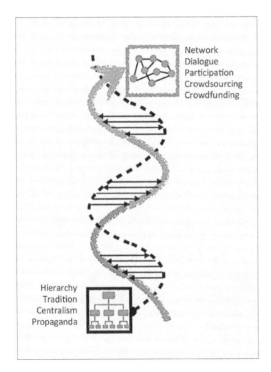

Figure 2. The helix as a model of shaping implementation instruments in the conditions of hybridization of governance and spatial management

Source: prepared by the author.

Conclusion

Today, hybridization of management is a widely used model of subjective relations in governance and public management. Processes based on highly complex relations and blurring of boundaries have become widespread and have marked their presence in contemporary theoretical models in spatial management. Understanding the benefits of creating complex relationships can also serve as a model for institutional change and related territorial shifts. It opens up new theoretical possibilities and perspectives for practical action.

The publication was financed from the subsidy granted to the Krakow University of Economics – Project nr 28/GGR/2021/POT.

References

Allmendinger P. and Haughton G. (2009). "Soft spaces, fuzzy boundaries, and metagovernance: The new spatial planning in the Thames Gateway". *Environment and Planning A: Economy and Space* 41, 617–633.

Andersen N.A. and Sand I.-J. (eds.). (2012). *Hybrid Forms of Governance: Self-suspension of Power*. London: Palgrave Macmillan.

Anheier H.K. and Krlev G. (2014). "Welfare regimes, policy reforms, and hybridity". *American Behavioral Scientist* 58(11), 1395–1411.

Boyer R. (1997). *Évolutions des modèles productifs et hybridation. Géographie, histoire et théorie*. Programme CEPREMAP, CNRS, E.H.E.S.S., No. 9804.

Camagni R. (2008). "Regional competitiveness: Towards a concept of territorial capital". In: *Modelling Regional Scenarios for the Enlarged Europe: European Competitiveness and Global Strategies*, R. Capello, R. Camagni, B. Chizzolini and U. Fratesi (eds.) (33–48). Berlin: Springer-Verlagu.

Camagni R., Caragliu A. and Perucca G. (2011). *Territorial Capital – Relational and Human Capital*. Politecnico di Milano. http://www.grupposervizioambiente.it/aisre/pendrive2011/pendrive/Paper/Camagni_Caragliu_Perucca.pdf. Accessed: 18.01.2023.

Carayannis E.G., Barth T.D. and Campbell D. (2012). "The Quintuple Helix innovation model: Global warming as a challenge and driver for innovation". *Journal of Innovation and Entrepreneurship* 1(2).

Czarniawska B. and Solli R. (2016). "Hybrydyzacja sektora publicznego". *Nordiske Organisa-sjonsstudier* 18(2), 23–36.

Drobniak A. (2019). "Definiowanie koncepcji hybrydyzacji rozwoju". *Rozwój Regionalny i Polityka Regionalna* 45, 23–40.

Elander I. (2002). *Partnerships and Urban Governance.* UNESCO 2002. Blackwell Publishers. http://www.sociologia.unimib.it/DATA/Insegnamenti/4_3037/materiale/elander.pdf.

Elsner W. (2004). "The 'new' economy: Complexity, coordination and a hybrid governance approach". *International Journal of Social Economics* 31(11–12), 1029–1049.

Etzkowitz H. and Leydesdorff L. (2000). "The dynamics of innovation: From National Systems and 'Mode 2' to a Triple Helix of university – industry – government relations". *Research Policy* 29, 109–123.

German L. and Keeler A. (2010). "Hybrid institutions: Applications of common property theory beyond discrete tenure regimes". *International Journal of the Commons* 4, 571–596.

Golubchikov O. (2016). "The urbanization of transition: Ideology and the urban experience". *Eurasian Geography and Economics* 57(4–5), 607–623.

Graham M. (2008). "Warped geographies of development: The Internet and theories of economic development". *Geography Compass* 2(3), 771–789. https://doi.org/10.1111/j.1749-8198.2008.00093.x.

Johanson J.E. and Vakkuri J. (2018). *Governing Hybrid Organisations: Exploring Diversity of Institutional Life.* London: Routledge (e-book).

Khana P. (2012). "The rise of hybrid governance". McKinsey Report.

Logvinov V. and Lebid N. (2018). "Is the smart cities of hybrid model of local government – the type III cities: Four possible answers". *Smart Cities and Regional Development Journal* 3, 9–30.

Mikuła Ł. (2019). *Zarządzanie rozwojem przestrzennym obszarów metropolitalnych w świetle koncepcji miękkich przestrzeni planowania.* Poznań: Uniwersytet im. Adama Mickiewicza w Poznaniu.

Miron D. and Gherasim I.A. (2018). "Linking the triple helix (university-industry-government) to the quadruple helix of university-industry-government – civil society in the field of international business and economics". *Proceedings of the 12^(th) International Conference on Business Excellence*, 612–625.

Noworól A. (2020). *Hybrydyzacja zarządzania rozwojem terytorialnym*. Warszawa: Wydawnictwo Naukowe Scholar.

Palej M. (2010). "Hybrydy – nowe elementy w strukturze miast". *Czasopismo Techniczne. Architektura* 14(107), 57–64.

Pieterse J.N. (2001). "Hybridity, so what?". *Theory, Culture & Society* 18(2–3), 219–245.

Rhodes R. (1997). *Understanding Governance: Policy Networks, Governance, Reflexivity and Accountability*. Buckingham: Open University Press.

Rifkin J. (2016). *The Zero Marginal Cost Society*. New York: Palgrave MacMillan.

Venturi R. (1966). *Complexity and Contradiction in Architecture*. New York: The Museum of Modern Art.

Wang G. and Yueh-yu Yeh E. (2005). "Globalization and hybridization in cultural products: The cases of Mulan and Crouching Tiger, Hidden Dragon". *International Journal of Cultural Studies* 8(2), 175–193. https://doi.org/10.1177/1367877905052416.

Maciej Teczke, Ph.D.
Jagiellonian University in Kraków

The implementation of flexible management methods in craft breweries: The impact on achieving competitive advantage in the brewing industry

Abstract

The article discusses the development of the craft beer market in Poland, and highlights the significance of organizational flexibility in achieving a competitive edge. In this paper, the author conducted a structured questionnaire among 31 craft breweries and presented the approach of Polish craft breweries to strategy, the pace of introducing new products, the tools most often used by breweries to enhance flexibility, as well as the directions for strategy modification.

Keywords: craft beer, management, flexibility, competitive advantage, brewing industry

Introduction

Beer has been one of the most popular stimulants in the world since 1980. The production of beer has doubled before 2016 (Szajner, 2019). From 2005 to 2018, consumption in Poland increased by 20 liters from 80.7 in 2005 to 100.5 in 2018 (Główny Urząd Statystyczny, n.d.). Until recently, this market was completely dominated by global concerns, which also applies to Poland (Drożdż, 2016). At the same time, there is a noticeable tendency in which the largest breweries are reducing their market share in favor of small and medium breweries (Szajner, 2019). The reason for this is the international development of craft brewing. The subject of craft brewing is increasingly noticeable in literature; however, it is relatively rarely directly related to the topic of management and its impact on the success of companies that operate in this industry. The article presents what influences the formulation of strategy by small breweries and reveals their perception on the importance of flexibility.

Brewing market

The last decade has been an extremely interesting time on the beer market. Both the world (Garavaglia and Swinnen, 2017) and Poland have seen a change called the "beer revolution". The beer revolution or the development of craft beers has its origins in the United States (Reid et al., 2014; Elzinga et al., 2015). The USA, which is still associated with poor quality beers from global corporations, underwent a revolution, thanks to which the number of breweries increased from 90 in 1980 to over 7450 in 2018 (Brewers Association, n.d. "National beer sales & production data"). In Poland, the beginning of the beer revolution is considered to be the launch of Pinta brewery and the release of a beer called "Attack of Hops" in the style of AIPA (American Indian Pale Ale) (Wojtyra, 2017). According to the data from the Polish Beer Map, in 2020 there were 262 active breweries in Poland (Piwna Mapa Polski – Moje Mapy Google, n.d.). At the same time there is a noticeable increase in the number of premieres of new beers each year. In 2014, this figure was 513 (Piwna Zwrotnica, n.d. "Piwne podsumowanie 2014"), while in 2019 this number increased to 2457 (Piwna Zwrotnica, n.d. "Piwne podsumowanie 2019"), which gives a nearly five-fold increase. Interestingly, the number of newly created breweries in this period is relatively constant and fluctuates around 50 new breweries each year, except for 2018 when 68 new plants (Wojtyra, 2017) were established. The goal of large breweries is to reach as many potential customers as possible with their product (Elzinga et al., 2017), which is why it must be universal. This is due to the effect of scale, which is necessary for large producers to compete. Craft breweries have chosen a different path in the form of small production of large quantities and high quality varied products.

There are different definitions of the term craft beer. T. Acitelli defines craft beer as follows: "This type of brewery includes any small, independently owned brewery that adheres to traditional brewing practices and ingredients. Craft brewers are distinct from larger regional and national breweries, which often use nontraditional ingredients and brew on a much vaster scale" (Acitelli, 2013), while the Brewers Association states:

> [...] small, independent and traditional. Small means brewing less than 6 million barrels per year, the federal limit for the small brewers excise tax exemption. Independent means that less than 25% of the brewery is owned by a non-craft brewer. Traditional refers to a focus on beers that are made entirely or mostly from malt, and not diluted with adjuncts like corn or rice (Brewers Association, n.d. "Craft brewer definition").

Small breweries are divided into three basic categories: microbreweries, contract breweries, and restaurant breweries. A contract brewery is an enterprise that does not have its own production capacity but is responsible for preparing the recipe, oversees the brewing process in the rented brewery, and handles the image, brand and logistics. A restaurant brewery is considered to be an enterprise that sells its product on site; this category also distinguishes brew pubs that sell their product on site as well, but it is not connected with an extensive gastronomic offer.

Enterprises, including breweries, that strive to implement flexible strategies which will allow them to react dynamically to changes in the environment, must be flexible. Here, flexibility is understood as an opportunity for the company to adapt its resources to changing operating conditions. This adjustment can be both quantitative and qualitative. Quantitative means that it is possible to quickly change the number of resources held, while qualitative relates to organizational changes that affect how resources are used. Therefore, flexibility of the enterprise will be the relation between the degree of risk associated with organizational shifts and the speed of response to introduced changes.

Most contemporary management concepts focus around making the organization's functions more flexible. An increasingly unpredictable environment requires companies to be able to adapt quickly to changes (Hamel, 2002). This requires the use of relatively simple instruments, such as leasing, outsourcing or flexible forms of employment, allowing the separation of some departments outside the organization, as well as comprehensive methods covering most areas of the enterprise's activity. However, because of the cost involved, attention is also drawn to the fact that flexibility cannot be an end in itself. In this case, the ability to adapt flexibility to needs becomes one of the key management skills (Teece et al., 2016).

One of R. Krupski's postulates regarding obtaining a flexible enterprise is redundancy, however, small- and medium-sized enterprises cannot afford this form of flexibility due to limited resources.

The biggest advantages of small and medium enterprises in the context of resource flexibility include a flat organizational structure, speed of decision making which affects the ability to use opportunities, and low inertia. A flat, non-hierarchical organizational structure, which departs from the functional approach, is increasingly becoming a key element in the literature that discusses affecting corporate flexibility. These elements appear in the concepts of lean management, agile management or process organizations, to name a few. Greater freedom in making decisions at lower management levels allows for faster response to environmental stimuli and for continuous improvement of processes. Such capacity for small and medium enterprises is definitely more attainable than for large ones. The main factors for which this is true is a lower inertia allowing for faster response and introduction of changes without incurring high costs, greater opportunities for employee participation in the functioning of the enterprise and definitely less formalization, which is often the main reason for the lack of quick response.

These opportunities are favored by the following features: a dynamic environment that rewards flexible companies which are capable of adapting and taking advantage of opportunities, and the development of modern management methods.

Increasing environmental turbulence means that the relative stability of the environment is less and less frequent, while decision uncertainty increases.

Quick response to changes is becoming one of the main factors allowing to gain competitive advantage. A high dynamics of change rewards enterprises that have created mechanisms allowing to minimize threats from the environment and to maximize opportunities. Achieving adaptive skills offers a chance in this respect. Here, adaptive skills are defined as the ability to integrate, build and reconstruct internal and external components to respond to changing surroundings (Teece et al., 1997).

However, a large number of threats to small- and medium-sized enterprises that have no effect on large competitors are also associated with the high dynamics of transformations. Factors such as the low stability of such organizations, lack of inventories and much smaller capital mean that every mistake made by small and medium enterprises can have much greater consequences. Most small and medium-sized enterprises cannot raise adequate capital, which is why a decrease in demand or other adverse random events can cause the company to collapse much faster than in the case of large corporations.

Empirical research

In order to conduct the study, we prepared a structured questionnaire consisting of 17 questions. The author sent about 150 questionnaires via e-mail and Messenger. In many cases, the author also conducted direct conversations during the Krakow BeerWeek 2019 craft festival. As a result, 31 completed questionnaires were received, producing a 20% return on surveys. At the same time, the sample constitutes 12% of the total population of craft breweries. However, limits have been introduced, which include the elimination of restaurant breweries and brewpubs that focus on local sales, and no larger-scale regional breweries were included. The questionnaires were filled in by persons with appropriate qualifications, i.e., owners and managers. Among the surveyed breweries, 16 were stationary and 14 were contract entities. The average employment in the surveyed companies is 7 people, and the enterprises are located all over Poland, without overrepresentation in one region.

The surveyed companies formulate short-term strategies. 68% of the surveyed enterprises focus on up to three years, while 13% for more than five years. When formulating their strategies, companies primarily take into

account the willingness to achieve their goals and focus on both the strength
nd weaknesses of the enterprise (Figure 1).

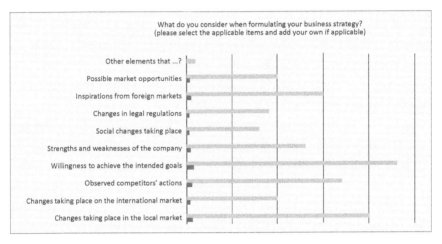

Figure 1. Formulating business strategy

Source: prepared by the author.

Interestingly, the surveye d companies draw inspiration from foreign
markets, while they take less ccount of the chages that occur there. A much
more important role is played by the changes that are local, which directly
affect the functioning of companies and often force the introduction of new
products or changes.

The most common reasons for introducing changes in the drawn up
strategy are detection of errors in the adopted assumptions, unsatisfactory
results of strategy implementation, and unexpected changes on the market
(Figure 2). These responses indicate that enterprises already have experience in correcting the assumed strategies, whether resulting from incorrect
assumptions or market shifts which were unpredictable during the formulation of the plan. What plays an extremely important role for this enterprise
group is flexibility (Figure 3). Among the surveyed enterprises, merely three
do not consider this feature significant. However, 38% of respondents indicated very high significance.

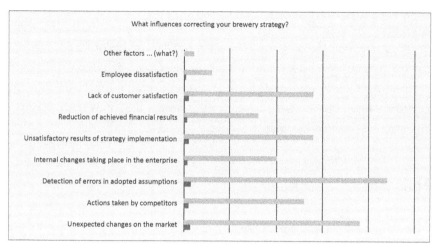

Figure 2. Correcting business strategy

Source: prepared by the author.

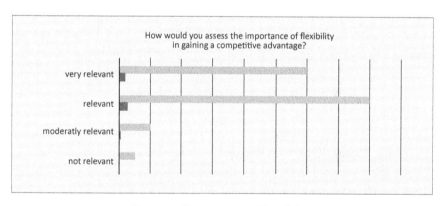

Figure 3. Importance of flexibility

Source: prepared by the author.

This trend is clearly seen in the number of new beers released annually. Craft breweries are definitely different from brewing concerns in this respect. What attracts customers is the significant diversity of the range and constant changes in the product portfolio. One example would be Pinta Brewery, which is running the "Pinta of the Month" campaign for yet another subsequent year, during which new beer is released every month, and some beers are later included in the regular offer. Until recently, corporations based almost exclusively on lagers and pilsners did not have such opportunities to offer new products – it was difficult in terms of production, but also at the corporate level. On the other hand, craft breweries that brew in small quantities can easily introduce new products.

Conclusion

The study has provided a better understanding of what factors influence the formulation and reformulation of strategy for small organisations operating in a highly dynamic environment.

The surveyed organisations, operating in a rapidly changing environment, need to demonstrate their ability to constantly change. Factors such as unexpected changes in the market or detected errors in assumptions were listed among the factors influencing changes in strategy. This indicates a high level of uncertainty and the difficulty in predicting whether assumptions made will come true.

The craft brewing market is characterised by the introduction of constant innovations, high customer awareness of the quality of the products offered and the need to react to what the competitors are doing and what the global trends are. These elements are noticeable in the survey conducted, where respondents point to such factors as: inspiration from foreign markets, changes taking place on the local market, actions taken by competitors or emerging opportunities in the environment. It is noticeable among the surveyed companies that practically all of them indicated that flexibility is important or very important, undoubtedly due to the characteristics of the industry in which they operate and which do not allow for a more static approach.

The environment forces small breweries to formulate strategies that incorporate flexibility and require adaptability. An immanent characteristic of craft breweries is constant change, adapting the range of products to customer expectations, which are changing dynamically. This sector shows how important it is today to be able to "change organisationally and to recognise upcoming changes from the environment.

The study presented indicates that the market studied forces organisations to act flexibly, taking into account changes resulting from the actions of competitors and requiring rapid adaptation to changing trends emerging both locally and internationally. Flexible management methods are in this case essential to remain competitive in the market.

References

Acitelli T. (2013). *The Audacity of Hops: The History of America's Craft Beer Revolution.* Chicago: Chicago Review Press.

Brewers Association (n.d.). "Craft brewer definition". https://www.brewersassociation.org/statistics-and-data/craft-brewer-definition/. Accessed: 17.01.2020.

Brewers Association. (n.d.). "National beer sales & production data". https://www.brewersassociation.org/statistics-and-data/national-beer-stats/. Accessed: 17.01.2020.

Drożdż J. (2016). *Ocena sytuacji ekonomiczno-finansowej przemysłu spożywczego w latach 2010–2014.* Warszawa: Dział Wydawnictw Instytutu Ekonomiki Rolnictwa i Gospodarki Żywnościowej.

Elzinga K.G., Tremblay C.H. and Tremblay V.J. (2015). "Craft beer in the United States: History, numbers, and geography". *Journal of Wine Economics* 10(3), 242–274. https://doi.org/10.1017/jwe.2015.22.

Elzinga K.G., Tremblay C.H., and Tremblay V.J. (2017). "Craft beer in the USA: Strategic connections to macro- and european brewers". In: *Economic Perspectives on Craft Beer: A Revolution in the Global Beer Industry*, C. Garavaglia and J. Swinnen (eds.) (55–88). Cham: Palgrave Macmillan. https://doi.org/10.1007/978-3-319-58235-1_2.

Garavaglia C. and Swinnen J. (eds.). (2017). *Economic Perspectives on Craft Beer: A Revolution in the Global Beer Industry.* Cham: Palgrave Macmilian. https://doi.org/10.1007/978-3-319-58235-1.

Główny Urząd Statystyczny (n.d.). "Dostawy na rynek krajowy oraz spożycie niektórych artykułów konsumpcyjnych na 1 mieszkańca w 2018 roku". https://stat.gov.pl/obszary-tematyczne/ceny-handel/handel/dostawy-na-rynek-krajowy-oraz-spozycie-niektorych-artykulow-konsumpcyjnych-na-1-mieszkanca-w-2018-roku,9,9.html. Accessed: 17.01.2020.

Hamel G. (2002). *Leading the Revolution: How to Thrive in Turbulent Times by Making Innovation a Way of Life*. New York: Plume.

Piwna Mapa Polski – Moje Mapy Google. (n.d.). https://www.google.com/maps/d/u/0/viewer?ll=50.80492749098491%2C19.520648516050073&spn=4.602969%2C8.843994&msa=0&mid=1H53727tGMjmaVg_8KJO9Mm63JJ8&z=8. Accessed: 17.01.2020.

Piwna Zwrotnica. (n.d.). "Piwne podsumowanie 2014". http://www.zwrotnica.com.pl/2014/12/piwne-podsumowanie-2014.html. Accessed: 17.01.2020.

Piwna Zwrotnica. (n.d.). "Piwne podsumowanie 2019". http://www.zwrotnica.com.pl/2020/01/piwne-podsumowanie-2019.html. Accessed: 17.01.2020.

Reid N., Mclaughlin R.B. and Moore M.S. (2014). "From yellow fizz to big biz: American craft beer comes of age". *Focus on Geography* 57(3), 114–125. https://doi.org/10.1111/foge.12034. 17.01.2020.

Szajner P. (2019). "Ewolucja światowego rynku piwa". *Zeszyty Naukowe SGGW w Warszawie – Problemy Rolnictwa Światowego* 18(33)(4), 60–68. https://doi.org/10.22630/prs.2018.18.4.97.17.01.2020.

Teece D.J., Pisano G. and Shuen, A. (1997). "Dynamic capabilities and strategic management". *Strategic Management Journal* 18(7), 509–533. https://doi.org/10.1002/(SICI)1097-0266(199708)18:7<509::AID-SMJ882>3.0.CO;2-Z.

Teece D., Peteratd M. and Leih S. (2016). "Dynamic capabilities and organizational agility". *California Management Review* 58(4), 4–9. https://doi.org/10.1525/cmr.2016.58.4.13.

Wojtyra B. (2017). "Rozwój przemysłu piwowarskiego w Polsce w okresie tzw. piwnej rewolucji w latach 2011–2016". *Problemy Zarządzania* 15(4), 107–123. https://doi.org/10.7172/1644-9584.75.6.

MICHAŁ TECZKE, PH.D.
Krakow University of Economics

The Internet of Things as a method of digitizing the consumer-manufacturer relationship

Abstract

The aim of the research is to identify the research gap in the field of Internet of Things research in the management sciences and empirically test consumer awareness of IoT. The author has carried out a general literature analysis and pointed to a research gap in the exploration of issues related to the Internet of Things in science management. The main area under consideration is focused on empirical operations, in which 525 people were examined using the CAWI method. The results and the conclusions drawn by the author are intended to indicate any potential paths that could be used by manufacturers of intelligent items to improve the consumer-manufacturer relationship. Progressive and all-encompassing digitization is, on the one hand, a great opportunity to accelerate communication processes, on the other hand it is a massive threat that is frightening to many customers. The author hopes that the presented results will be the nucleus of further considerations and will enable seeking a more complete picture in the future.

Keywords: IoT, consumer-manufacturer relationship, consumer feedback, data security

Introduction

J. McCarthy is considered the father of artificial intelligence. In the mid-1950s, McCarthy defined artificial intelligence as the science and engineering of intelligent machines, in particular smart computer programs that enabled the use of computers to understand human intelligence (Malucha, 2018, p. 53). The concept of the Internet of Things (IoT) evolved from the activities initiated in the 1950s and aimed at creating artificial intelligence in the late 1990s. It was first used in 1999 by K. Asthon during the presentation of Procter & Gamble. As the creator of the discussed issue notes (Asthon, 2010, p. 7), the combination of RFID (radio-frequency identification), which was modern at that time, and the possibilities offered by using the Internet, was much more than just an attempt to raise the interest of the management board. At present, the idea has found a permanent place in business in functional and political terminology (e.g., the Digital Single Market Strategy proposed by the European Commission). In its nature, the Internet of Things is explored with particular intensity in areas related to computer science and the application of tools used in communication, however, more and more often it is taken up by scientists dealing with other disciplines, including economics and management. The Internet of Things uses RFID radio identification systems as well as sensor systems that allow computer systems to observe, identify and analyze the environment and individual objects with much greater accuracy than could result from human intervention. This can be compared to an autopilot in an airplane, which is much more effective in analyzing data than the pilot himself (Smejda, 2016, p. 43). In the case of manufacturing processes, a number of systems can be distinguished that can potentially become an intermediary between the information channel and the physical environment. Naturally, in order to become "things" in the context of the Internet of Things, they must be equipped with a network card (cable or wireless) and information encoding devices in the standard accepted by computer networks (Lipski, 2015, p. 756). Data can be collected through the use of the Internet of Things by means of many methods and channels. As a result, data is obtained and analyzed in real time, which makes it easier to make management decisions at every level (starting with individual users and ending with managing compiled ecosystems). Any item or device (called a "thing" or "smart item") in the networks of the Internet of Things can automatically connect to the Internet, being a full-fledged node of the network, and communicate with any other item (device) connected to it. In practice, this communication is sometimes limited at the level of access authorization and assignment of specific rights (Mącik, 2016, p. 13). The structure of network connections and the organization of IoT networks at various levels is highly distributed and dynamic. It consists of "smart" network nodes / modules that generate data for the network, as well as receive and process information (Ożadowicz, 2014, p. 88). Robotization and automation eliminate the direct participation of employees in the production process and reduce it to the role of general supervision. In the Industry 4.0, fully automated production lines supported by robots are connected to the world of IT and the Internet of Things, i.e., ubiquitous access to data and information (Założeń et al., 2018). Billions of devices, connected in the network thanks to the Internet of Things, generate huge amounts of data in an extremely short period of time. The data should be collected for further analysis and processing in the cloud (Bojanowska, 2019, p. 2). According to the information presented by the analytical company McKinsey Digital, by 2025 the use of the Internet of Things in nine key branches (home, offices, production, sales automation, work, health, logistics, city and vehicles) will have generated estimated impact in the range from 3.9 to 11.1 trillion dollars (Manyika et al., 2015, p. 9). It is estimated that currently the number of devices connected to the Internet has exceeded 26.5 billion (Techjury.net, 2019). The items are not "anonymous", but function in an intelligent network that provides for the possibility of unequivocal identification and enables automatic communication and cooperation. This network leads to numerous benefits that cannot be achieved by other methods. On the other hand, there are many problems that need to be solved (Kobyliński, 2014, p. 102). Hence, the purpose of this article is to attempt to provide a solution for the progressive digitization of business relationships between customers and manufacturers.

Current research on the Internet of Things from the perspective of management sciences

In order to determine the research gap, the author analyzed data on the frequency of the term "Internet of Things" in scientific publications classified in SCOPUS databases from the first use by K. Asthon in 1999 until the end of 2019. The results are presented in Figure 1.

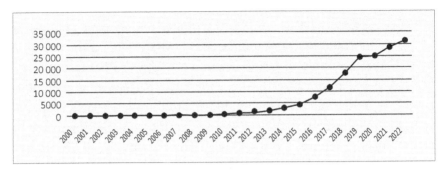

Figure 1. Number of articles containing the phrase "Internet of Things" in 2000–2021

Source: prepared by the author.

Clearly, the issue is readily used for scientific research. In the years indicated, 160 025 documents were registered in the SCOPUS database, of which as many as 126 636 in the past five years (representing over 79% of all documents), 60% of documents in the analyzed database are conference materials and 32% are scientific articles. It can definitely be confirmed that this issue is not only current, but also the interest in it is increasing every year. While the issue is interesting and willingly explored, the vast majority of research is carried out in the field of technical sciences, as shown in Figure 2. As can be seen, most published scientific texts concern computer science (36.0%) and engineering (23.53%), while only 6898 scientific publications were published in the area of business, economics and accounting, which translates into 2.4% of all analyzed texts. It is worth noting that more scientific publications related to the Internet of Things have been presented in such academic fields as energy and social sciences. In the author's opinion, the area of issues related to the Internet of Things considered from a management perspective requires in-depth exploration by subsequent authors.

To conclude, it should be emphasized once again that the subject of the considerations is very current and a further increase in its popularity can be expected in the coming years. However, despite the fact that the issues refer to information sciences, the ubiquity of devices that use the Internet of Things technology allows to conclude that the effects of their use are well seen in other areas of science, including management and quality sciences.

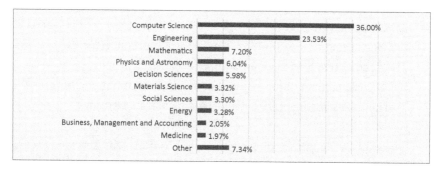

Figure 2. Documents by subject area

Source: prepared by the author.

Methodical assumptions

The main aim of the study is to examine the attitudes and behavior of consumers with particular emphasis on the potential of the Internet of Things in order to improve the relationship between consumers and manufacturers. The main research problem was to find the answer to the question: "Do consumers willingly use the Internet of Things to improve the consumer-manufacturer relationship?". In order to find a satisfactory solution, the author used partial questions:

1) Do consumers want products that fully meet their needs?
2) Do consumers feel the need for sharing opinions on the degree of satisfying their needs with manufacturers?
3) What are consumers most afraid of when using the Internet of Things to provide feedback on the degree of satisfaction with the use of devices?

The research questions are accompanied by corresponding hypotheses. The main hypothesis was defined: "Consumers would be willing to use the Internet of Things to improve the consumer-manufacturer relationship, but they have limited awareness of its benefits as well as concerns about data security". The following partial hypotheses to the partial questions were presented:

1) Consumers definitely want products to precisely meet their needs,
2) Consumers do not want to share information on the level of satisfying their needs with manufacturers,
3) The main concern regarding the use of the Internet of Things is the fear of disclosing private data to inappropriate entities.

The study was conducted on a group of 525 adults with access to the Internet. The study was carried out using the Computer-Assisted Web Interview (CAWI). The sample selection was unrepresentative and purposeful. Most of the respondents were students of (first and second degree) university studies in the Lesser Poland Region (the Krakow University of Economics, AGH University of Krakow, Jagiellonian University in Kraków and the State Higher Vocational School in Nowy Sącz). Despite the lack of representativeness of the studied sample, the conclusions drawn from the study are interesting and can certainly provide the basis for further, expanded research. Participation was fully arbitrary and did not involve any benefits for students. The analysis was not preceded by preliminary information regarding neither the subject nor the scope of the empirical study.

Basic data on the structure of the research sample is presented in Figure 3. As can be seen, the distribution of the gender structure was more or less even with a slight predominance of women (44.33%) over men (55.67%). Because the survey was purposeful, the age of the overwhelming majority (87.63%) was predicted to be between 18 and 25 years old. The oldest respondent participating in the survey was 55 years old. There was one optional question regarding the wealth of the respondents. From a pool of 525 people surveyed, 4 people did not respond to the question. Over half of the respondents considered their material position good (53.4%), less than a third (31.13%) indicated the response "average", 12.99% indicated a very good financial standing, and 1.65% – a poor one. None of the respondents indicated their position as "very bad".

The last criterion presenting the structure of the division of respondents was the place of residence, which seems to be the most diverse. The largest number of respondents (30.72%) live in villages. The second most frequently indicated result (30.72%) was a city with over 500,000 inhabitants. Further places indicate a city with less than 200,000 inhabitants (20.62%) and a city between 200,000 and 500,000 inhabitants (4.95%).

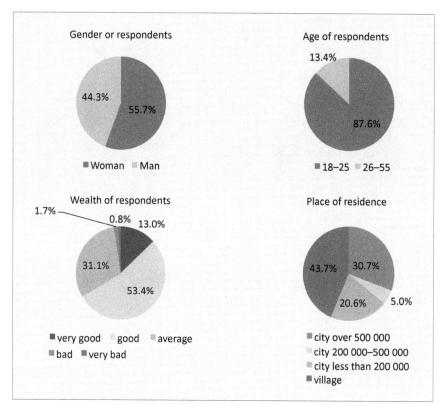

Figure 3. Basic data on the structure of the research sample

Source: prepared by the author.

Results of the study

The first questions in the survey concerned recognition of the concept of the Internet of Things. Given that the vast majority of young people have participated in higher education systems, the author expected a considerable percentage of positive responses. The results, however, indicated a different state. Over 75% of respondents said that they had never encountered this concept before. It is also worth noting that a significant proportion of participants who indicated a positive response are first degree students of engineering.

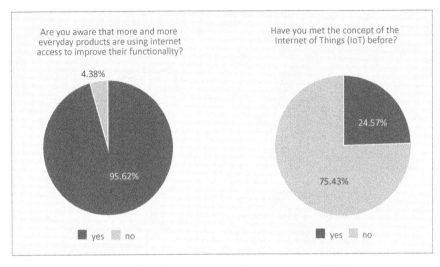

Figure 4. Knowledge of the concept of the Internet of Things among respondents

Source: prepared by the author.

However, the prevailing ignorance is merely limited to the concept itself. The general essence of the Internet of Things functionality is known to over 95% of respondents.

Further questions were already related directly to the research problems indicated earlier. As expected, respondents definitely want their products to meet their expectations. Almost 85% agreed with the statement that "Manufacturers should use all possibilities to adjust their product to the expectations of recipients" on the 5-point Likert scale. Detailed results are presented in Figure 5. The responses directly confirm the first partial hypothesis. As expected by the researcher, consumers not only want products to exactly match their needs, but even think that manufacturers should use the methods and tools available to them to continuously improve their goods and to adapt them to the changing tastes and needs. This statement is by no means revealing, however, its relation to the potential of the Internet of Things and the possibility of automating machine communication processes results in further conclusions, which will be presented later in this discussion.

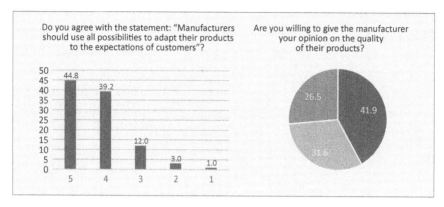

Figure 5. Should manufacturers adapt the product to the expectations of consumers and do you provide feedback? (result in % of responses)

Source: prepared by the author.

Another issue examined was the willingness to provide feedback. The survey demonstrated that 41.90% of respondents never provide feedback regarding the degree of satisfaction with the device used. Another 31.62% provided only information about their dissatisfaction, and 26.48% were willing to provide details about their satisfaction or a suggestion to improve functionality. It can be concluded that the two responses indicate a specific dichotomy in consumer perception, namely there is a strong tendency to claiming that manufacturers should take care of matching products to consumer needs, while not being willing to share information about whether the consumers themselves are satisfied with the product. Manufacturers could use the possibilities of the Internet of Things to analyze how their devices are used. Constantly connected to the Internet, TV sets, mobile phones, refrigerators, vacuum cleaners, cars and thousands of other devices could provide information about the frequency of use, load of individual components, and instructions given by the owner. Certainly, this would allow to adapt devices to the tasks faced by their consumers.. The question that must be asked is whether consumers would voluntarily allow devices to send such information to their manufacturers. The study indicates that there is a relatively high resistance to such activity. The results presented in Figure 6 show that in the case of automation of reporting pure technical parameters (e.g., power consumption, component loads, etc.), the supporters and opponents of such a solution are divided almost equally. When information such as details about the peripherals connected to the product, how often and in what way the device is used, are added to the pool of the analyzed parameters, the number of opponents of such a solution increases sharply, with 69.3% being against it and merely 27.2% speaking in favor of it.

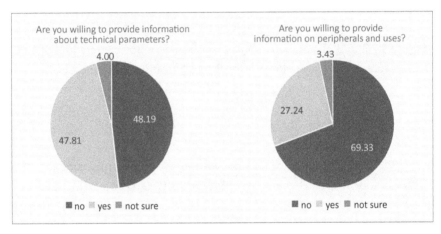

Figure 6. Are you willing to provide information regarding technical parameters and ways of use? (result in % of responses)

Source: prepared by the author.

The analysis of the results presented above demonstrates that the second partial hypothesis has not been fully confirmed. Depending on the type of information that would be transferred via the Internet of Things from consumers to manufacturers, acceptance of such activity varies significantly. In the case of providing information on pure technical parameters, one can find a fairly large group of consumers who consider such action to be positive. The hypothesis becomes stronger if consumers provide information on how to use the product. In this situation, a significant proportion of respondents do not agree to sending this type of information to manufacturers. If so, what is the greatest barrier? And what are the possibilities of breaking it? In searching for the answer to the question, what are the people who use objects that automatically access the Internet most afraid of? The most frequent responses were surveillance, loss of private data, hacking intrusions, virus infection of devices, and unlawful use of data. A qualitative representation of the most frequently repeated fears is presented in Figure 7. The conclusions drawn from the considerations simultaneously confirm the third partial hypothesis. In fact, the loss of private data or uncontrolled access to private information is considered by the respondents as the greatest fear associated with the use of devices that automatically gain access to the Internet.

Figure 7. The most common concerns about the Internet of Things

Source: prepared by the author.

As shown, the loss of control over private data in the analyzed population is the greatest and loudest-articulated fear, therefore should it not be considered as the main barrier limiting the possibility of using the Internet of Things to digitize consumer-manufacturer relations? According to the author, it is precisely this risk area that manufacturers should minimize by presenting real and specific ways to counteract undesirable interference by providing a certainty of security and perhaps offering the clients various benefits for the ability to analyze certain information.

Conclusion

In conclusion, it can be stated that the main research hypothesis that "Consumers would be willing to use the Internet of Things to improve the consumer-manufacturer relationship, but they have limited awareness of the benefits of this and have concerns about data security", has been confirmed. The analyzed group strongly emphasizes the need for manufacturers to adapt to consumer expectations. At the same time, there is a kind of dichotomy due to the fact that respondents are not willing to provide feedback on the degree of satisfaction from buying a product. This can be explained by the progressing digitization and the growing accustomation of recipients to the fact that things "happen by themselves", often without the explicit will of the users. Consumers willingly transfer the necessity of obtaining full feedback to the manufacturers, not engaging in providing feedback at all. It seems that manufacturers, who clearly want to obtain the largest number of reliable feedbacks, could use this gap to build a healthy partnership between themselves and the customers. The most important step along this path is, without a doubt, a clear definition of what information they would like to receive and how they want to use it. Because any intelligent item can be easily and precisely identified, one can imagine creating specific loyalty applications in which users could preview groups of information that have been passed to manufacturers. Perhaps, depending on the degree of commitment to the process of improving the product quality, users allowing access to specific data could count on certain benefits (e.g., small discounts on other products, the opportunity to take part in online sales or presales, the possibility of faster and more personalized contact customer service, or other). The potential benefits for each party cannot be overestimated. On the one hand, consumers who provide information would be rewarded for their attitude, while on the other, manufacturers would gain access to much more details about the degree of customer satisfaction and ways of using the purchased products. It is obvious that increasing the degree of independent consumer activity would directly translate into a reduction in the costs incurred by companies in order to obtain this information by means of more traditional methods.

In order to even consider building such a relationship, the first and most important step that must be made by manufacturers is to recognize the consumers' concerns as justified and to attempt to solve them. The author that the greatest role in this aspect is played by the so-called GAFA (Google, Amazon, Facebook, Apple), the largest cyber-corporation. Unfortunately, consumers often receive information about an overt violation of partner relations. There have been cases such as the lawsuit against VIZIO in the United States, which carried out surveillance of their consumers through smart TVs without customers' consent. According to the court's application, the company, which is one of the world's largest TV manufacturers, obtained 100 billion different information each day without the consent of customers, using 11 million connected television sets. It should be strongly emphasized that the solution to this type of practice is not to force the user to accept a license with a hidden consent to downloading data. The only acceptable form of building healthy relationships is partnership and treating customers with the respect they deserve. As long as manufacturers strive to download data without clearly specifying what information they download and for what purpose, there is no chance of partnership. Such activities over a long period of time can only cause more and more efforts on the part of customers to tightly secure themselves against providing any information. It can be seen, however, that such processes have already begun, as an increasing number of people want to "disappear" from the Internet, and users are more and more often turning towards TOR browsers (providing the highest degree of anonymity).

The author would like to emphasize once again that the research sample was intentional, and the conclusions can only serve as a catalyst for further reflection on the indicated topic. However, the fact that a significant proportion of respondents are young educated people enables us to expect that the observed phenomena are not individual and will be more and more visible in the future.

References

Asthon K. (2010). "That 'Internet of Things' Thing". *RFID Journal* 22, 97–114.

Bojanowska A. (2019). "Customer data collection with Internet of Things". *MATEC Web of Conferences*, 252. https://doi.org/10.1051/matecconf/201925201001.

Kobyliński A. (2014). "Internet przedmiotów: szanse i zagrożenia". *Zeszyty Naukowe Uniwersytetu Szczecińskiego* 7(808), 101–109.

Lipski J. (2015). "Internet rzeczy w zastosowaniu do sterowania produkcją". *Innowacje w Zarządzaniu i Inżynierii Produkcji* 2, 755–766.

Malucha M. (2018). "Internet of things – the technological context and areas of application". *Studia i Prace WNEiZ* 54, 51–69.

Manyika J., Chui M., Bisson P., Woetzel J., Dobbs R. and Bughin D.A. (2015). "The Internet of Things: Mapping the value beyond". McKinsey & Company. https://www.mckinsey.com/business-functions/digital-mckinsey/our-insights/the-internet-of-things-the-value-of-digitizing-the-physical-world. Accessed: 22.03.2020.

Mącik R. (2016). "'Internet rzeczy' – postrzegane przez młodych konsumentów korzyści i zagrożenia – wyniki badań wstępnych". *Przedsiębiorczość i Zarządzanie* 17, 11–27.

Ożadowicz A. (2014). "Internet Rzeczy w systemach automatyki budynkowej". *Napędy i Sterowanie* 12, 88–93.

Smejda P. (2016). "Internet rzeczy (IoT) we współczesnej gospodarce. Rola, zadania i bariery rozwoju". *Zeszyty Naukowe. Organizacja i Zarządzanie* 64, 43–57.

Techjury.net. (2019). "How many IoT devices are there in 2019? More than ever!". https://techjury.net/blog/how-many-iot-devices-are-there/#gref. Accessed: 14.02.2020.

Założeń P.I., Gajdzik B. and Grabowska S. (2018). "Modele biznesowe w przedsiębiorstwach 4.0 użytych do wyznaczenia nowych modeli biznesu". *Zarządzanie Przedsiębiorstwem. Enterprise Management* 21(3), 2–8. https://doi.org/10.15611/zp.2018.3.01.

Agnieszka Thier, Ph.D.
Krakow University of Economics

Succession as a key element of sustainable development in a family-owned business

Abstract

A paper presenting the opinions of a wide range of practitioners speaks for the development of a specific organizational culture and social responsibility of family businesses. Succession and the longevity of a family business can raise some formal, organizational, financial or even psychological barriers. However, longevity represents a certain value that cannot be converted into acquires above. Entrepreneurs who have successfully gone through succession see a fundamental value in the longevity of their company. The advantage of family businesses is the long-term orientation of business activity and the desire to pass the business on to descendants. In the functioning of such an enterprise, "family logic" often dominates over "business logic", family values over economic values. Such properties of family enterprises are closely correlated with the concept of sustainable socio-economic development, which is widely promoted today.

Keywords: family business, succession, plan of succession, family constitution, longevity, sustainable development

Introduction

Succession in a family business means a generational change involving the transfer of ownership, power and knowledge by its previous owner and manager (nestor) to his successor, provided that the family character of the company is preserved. It is transferring responsibilities (rights and duties, knowledge resources related to the management of the company) from the nestor to the successor. The primary intention of succession is to ensure the development of the family business and its survival in the market. We can define a successor as a member of the owner family in the second or next generation, who prepares for the generational change and works in the family business (PARP, 2014; Bar, 2018).

Today there are over 800,000 family businesses in Poland, accounting for approximately 90% of all business entities in the country. Over 261,000 people work in the top 100 largest family businesses in Poland. Today 2.4 million owners are registered in the Central Register and Information on Economic Activity (CEIDG). Approx. 520 thousand of them are over 60 years old (Ministerstwo Rozwoju i Technologii, 2023; Thier, 2020). Most of these people will soon face the need for succession.

Until recently, in Western Europe, the founders' children took only 30% of family businesses over, 10–12% was taken over by grandchildren and only 3–5% by great-grandchildren (Family Business Yearbook, 2015; Deloitte, 2016). According to more recent data, the 2nd generation now takes over 50% of family businesses, while the 3rd generation takes over 25%. This growth is partly because of consolidation of the family business sector. However, the dominant model of development is still one in which the 1st generation builds the company, the 2nd generation sustains and grows the business, while the 3rd generation squanders the assets, sells them, or restructures by turning the company into a joint-stock company (Family Business, 2023; KPMG, 2020; Thier, 2020; Thinktank, 2018).

In the second half of the XX century, there was a "business over-mortality" in the world. In this period, ⅓ of large enterprises ceased to exist after just 20–30 years and ½ of large multinational corporations after 70 years (Cipiur, 2019). Today, despite the fact that 70–80% of company founders in Poland wish to pass their enterprise to their descendants, half of them do not have a proper plan to do so (Deloitte, 2016; Romanowska, 2017). According to a recent survey conducted in Małopolska, 45% of family businesses are planning succession in the next 10 years. Only 32% of them have taken the first steps towards it, like a discussion within the family or getting information on succession mechanisms, only 14% of companies have a succession plan prepared (Urząd Marszałkowski w Krakowie, 2023). The current problem, therefore, is the effective succession of a family business. The reasons for failed successions are various, and include family misunderstandings, lack of interest from potential successors or the cost of taking over the inheritance (Małyszek, 2011).

Unification of succession rules is being handled by the European Commission. During of every decade new owners take 20–40% of European companies over. Every year, over 650,000 companies with about 3 million employees undergo the succession process in the EU. In 1993, the European Commission organized the 1ˢᵗ EU Symposium on Generational Change in Family Business. In 1994, guidelines were planned on the principles of ownership transfer in small and medium-sized family businesses. In 2003, a manual of good practices for business transfers was published. In 2007, the Expert Group on Family Business was established (European Commission, 1994, 2003, 2009). According to its assessments, the younger generation is less and less interested in taking over the family business. Therefore, succession planning was recommended to include the option of selling the business to third parties. Also, the issue of succession was taken up in Poland by the Entrepreneurship Council (Ministry of Economy). In 2016, PARP launched a program to support the succession of family businesses. The result of the efforts of these two institutions was the Law on Succession Management of a Natural Person's Business (PARP, 2016; Sejm RP, 2018). Because of a corresponding amendment to PIT and CIT taxes, depreciation of the inherited business was restored from the initial value (Sejm RP, 2017). This was important for heirs of single-person family businesses. As with donations, depreciation is now continued by the recipient. Drafts of other legislation and analytical and consulting work have also been undertaken.

The adoption of a family business creates new opportunities for the successor. Because of his younger age or better education compared to his predecessor (greater professionalism and innovation), the new manager can create the right conditions for the development of the family business. Performing an effective succession allows a family business to come closer to becoming a long-lived enterprise. A business that has existed for at least 100 years can be put into the category of such establishments (Goto, 2014). Effective successions lead to an increase in the number of long-lived family businesses, resulting in an increase in the share of such companies in the economy (Kuta et al., 2017; Więcek-Janka, 2013; Wojewoda, 2019).

Objective and subjective difficulties in succession performing

Succession is a key moment in the life of a family business often determining its future. The need for succession can arise for a variety of reasons: the owner reaching retirement age and the need to transfer power to the younger generation; the owner's ill health; divorce; a change in the owner's professional or social interests; changes in the market situation of the industry or in legislation that can be better handled by a younger successor; other fortuitous situations (Lewandowska et al., 2015). Sources of uncertainty at this stage of the enterprise's life are threats or opportunities related to changes in management and management system. At the same time, in a non-family business, changes in management are usually gradual, such as at the will of shareholders or the board of directors. Succession results in changes in the ownership structure and management style of the family business. However, the participants in this process strive to preserve the values important to the family and to the industry of the business in question (Jeżak, 2014; Lewandowska, 2015).

The succession process is natural, but it must be prepared by the family and then properly planned by the nestor and the company's management. This usually turns out to be more difficult than running a company. The difficulties concern not only the formal side, but also the psychological dimension. There is talk of a succession paradox, when the founder declares the transfer of the company to a successor, but does not make adequate efforts, delaying the final decision (Leach, 2017). As a result, the plan to perform the ownership and power transferring is often late or contains serious flaws. It also often happens that an establishment has no documented succession plan. The owner of a family business usually wants to maintain power for as long as possible, mainly out of fear of retirement. Also, sometimes he delays succession in the face of difficulties in selecting a successor. Similar indecision often finds understanding in the spouses or children of the nestor. They may have concerns about their own ability to run the company. Also, it is often the case that company's employees are emotionally attached to the boss and fear the changes associated with a new CEO (Dźwigoł-Barosz, 2017). Sometimes the nestor wishes to share power with a successor as an advisor, or even manage in an autocratic manner. Also, trouble can arise from the fact that the company is run by 2–3 owners (such as a married couple or siblings).

Children or other family members may not be interested in taking over the company, especially if they are not properly prepared substantively and psychologically. The successor, after taking over the management, changes his professional and material status and sometimes lifestyle and social position (Hutcheson, 2022). For the above reasons, family business associations recommend preparing a written succession plan.

During the period of succession, strategic risks to the company may become apparent. They arise mainly from the change of the person in charge of the company and the resulting concerns among suppliers and customers about the continuity of management, previous market policies and the treatment of business partners. Similar uncertainties may also arise among the employees of the family business in question. Therefore, during the succession period, the nestor and then his successor should declare loyalty to the company's traditions, values, strategies and priorities. This attitude is worth communicating to all stakeholders associated with the company. This is best done in writing.

Other barriers to succession are the lack of practices and patterns for carrying out transfers of assets and power. Most Polish family businesses were established after 1990, so the tradition of drawing up detailed succession plans is still a new phenomenon in Poland. In small enterprises, there is an often reluctance by the leader to external advisors or lack of time for these matters. That is why company statutes or articles of association say little on the subject. However, now the situation changing because of the self-organization of family businesses and the relevant activities of, among others, the Polish Agency for Enterprise Development, the Ministry of Enterprise and Technology and auditing and consulting firms. The promotion of thoughtful succession is also promoted by many publications (Kuta et al., 2017; Małyszek, 2011; PARP, 2014, 2016, 2018; Piekarski and Rudzińska, 2012; Surdej and Wach, 2010; Wojewoda, 2019).

Ways to improve the process of succession of a family business

In the legislation of various countries, normative facilitation of succession is emerging. The first step in this direction in Poland was the adoption of the legal act facilitating succession in the establishment of an individual (Sejm RP,

2018). Up to now, the death of the owner meant the cessation of the legal existence of the enterprise. Now the matter is taken over by a successor administrator. The next step was the enactment of the Family Foundation Law, which avoids the fragmentation of assets and ensures the uninterrupted operation of the business and succession (Ministerstwo Przedsiębiorczości i Technologii, 2019; Sejm RP, 2023). Currently, some owners of large family businesses are trying to establish foundations abroad, as in Poland they can only operate for a social or public purpose and not for a private one (for the benefit of the family).

In Poland, various aspects of the succession process are covered by family law, inheritance law, civil law, business and commercial law, and administrative law. The law clarifies issues of ownership in marriage, ownership over real estate and the legal form of a business. In addition, the law establishes rules for the disposition of a business in terms of sale, donation, inheritance and maintenance of management in the event of divorce or death. The legislation displays ways to change the legal form of the business under these circumstances (Marjański, 2016). Five legal steps in the succession process can be distinguished:

- Timely decision to start succession planning;
- Discernment of the property regime of the spouses;
- Choosing the method of transferring the business by donation, sale (more commonly used in the West) or inheritance after the owner's death;
- Analyzing whether statutory inheritance is compatible with the chosen succession model (e.g., who inherits and in what proportions);
- Preparation of wills (especially when there is no succession plan yet).

A succession plan should specify how ownership will change and how management will be transferred (Rothwell and Prescott, 2023; Ramadani et al., 2020). To a large extent, such a plan depends on the legal form of the family business. The most popular form is an individual business (an establishment of an individual), which, however, poses the greatest problems in the succession process. This is because, in this case, the founder is responsible for his assets for the liabilities incurred. Therefore, the 'business method' is recommended, i.e., launching a new company, which will gradually take over the assets during the temporary (6–24 months) and parallel operation of both entities. Then the existing company is liquidated. Other possible options are: sale of the company for the market price after agreement with creditors; donation with tax consideration; in-kind contribution of all assets to the new company; conversion into a limited liability or joint stock company. With a partnership, there is a similar predicament, since such an enterprise is managed by several partners. The easiest way to perform succession is in a commercial company. Experience shows that a contingency plan is necessary, and you should start there. After all, resolving the details of a succession plan takes quite a long time, especially in large families. Therefore, it is advisable to protect against emergencies by drawing up wills in advance, excluding the inheritance of shares, using financial instruments (such as life insurance policies).

The economic aspects of a succession are important because of issues such as sources of funding for the process, valuing the business, making sure taxes are paid, settling accounts with siblings who do not include shares, and ensuring the financial stability of the doyenne for retirement. This means an increase in the cost of operating the business, which can threaten its liquidity. Therefore, a financial plan for succession must be prepared in advance. It must be linked to the economic condition of the business (which should be reasonably good). In addition, for organizational and financial reasons, the process of generational change is worth spreading over time.

The basis for preparing the economic part of the succession plan is the valuation of the enterprise. In doing so, it is necessary to consider the value of resources included in the balance sheet and off-balance sheet resources. The latter includes the skills and loyalty of employees, the quality of production and service technologies, the customer base and their opinions about the company. To a certain extent, the company's balance sheet says this as a pledge of fixed and current assets and liabilities divided into equity and liabilities. Among them, we distinguish buildings, structures and other real estate, machinery and equipment, tools, intangible assets, patents, inventories, cash, receivables. The second important financial document is the profit-and-loss account (income statement), with a breakdown of sales revenue and operating expenses, as well as profit (loss) and income tax. Based on these statements and other factors, a valuation of the enterprise is performed, adjusted to the succession conditions and analytical possibilities.

The basic and simple method of valuation is the asset method, which involves estimating the value of assets and subtracting the value of debt from it. Accounting valuation is then the easiest. It is done based on business books, and considers the cost of purchasing and installing the asset, possibly with depreciation. Over time, because of inflation, such a valuation has a very preliminary, general character. Therefore, the asset method can use an adjustment by using current asset prices. However, this method is very labor-intensive. The income method is considered better. Here, the value of the enterprise is calculated primarily based on its economic effects (financial result). This uses a discount calculus, which fully takes into consideration the time factor. This is essential in calculating the economic efficiency of investments. Listed companies use the PE (price-earnings ratio) as a ratio of the market price of shares and net profit. For larger companies, it is worth consulting external experts. Proportionate and consistent with statutory inheritance, the distribution of assets in family businesses avoids adverse financial consequences. Otherwise, the children of the nestor outside the company who are not included in the above distribution may have to be allocated property of the nestor outside the company or be awarded a retainer.

The human life cycle determines the likely timing of succession. Therefore, a plan for this process developed in advance facilitates due preparation of the business and its owner for the generational change. It is advisable to educate children and other family members in the company's spirit values as early as the establishment of the business. Beside this, it is advisable to prepare the successor in terms of content and psychology to take over assets and power. A succession plan drawn up in time makes it easier to resolve issues of doubt and controversy. Such a problem may be the existence of several successor candidates or the lack of a suitable candidate (Hutcheson, 2022). In the latter case, the sale of the business may come into play, ensuring financial security for the owner and harmony within the family. The second solution is to transfer power to a manager from outside the family. It is recommended in the situation of a large number of relatives, which usually occurs in families of third or next generation business owners (Leach, 2017).

An entrepreneur at the head of a family business must appreciate the importance of succession and prepare a plan to carry out ownership, power and knowledge transferring into the hands of a successor (Piekarski and

Rudzińska, 2012). The absence of such a succession plan can introduce chaos into the operation of the business, become the cause of slowing down production or sales, and even bankrupt the company. Despite this, many family businesses do not have a succession plan. The reasons for this are neglecting or postponement to the matter, lack of interest from potential successors, lack of appropriate qualifications in successors (Deloitte, 2016).

The succession plan should specify how the business will be handed over, determining the family's influence on the process; the next steps and costs of carrying out the generational change; the strategy and vision of the business for the future. The plan should also specify the responsibilities of the owner, employees and the successor during and after the succession; a list of necessary legal and financial documents; the succession schedule. The succession process involves not only the nestor and successor but also the co-owners of the business, other family members and employees of the company. Indirectly, the process also affects the company's suppliers and customers, so it is worth informing them about the generational change in their contractor's company.

Longevity of the family businesses as a value

The successor's assumption of the functions of owner and CEO is carried out gradually under the supervision of the predecessor, the Family Council or the Supervisory Board. Only after a certain period does the successor assume full responsibility. However, in small companies, such a change can occur immediately after the preparation of documents. Thoughtful succession is a process that sometimes lasts for the several years needed to prepare the company and its new leader for change. To ensure that there are no conflicts within the owners' family during this period, the rules of generational change must be transparent (Lewandowska 2015; Lewandowska and Lipiec, 2015, 2021; Lewandowska, 2021; Lewandowska et al., 2015; May and Lewandowska, 2021). A Family Constitution can serve this purpose, which should be prepared and adopted well before the succession process begins. Family constitutions can refer to the company's history, its mission and future strategy, operating principles and the company's values. In addition, a family constitution specifies issues like (i) succession and shareholder agreements, (ii) dividends, (iii) company valuation, and (iv) management structure. According to data conducted, drafting a constitution helps maintain the continuity of a family business across generations (Ramadani et al., 2020).

Some authors emphasize the correlation that occurs between the stages of life of the founder (owner) and the phases of development of a particular family business. D. Levinson distinguished 8 life stages correlated with the logic of business development. These include the stage of implementation in the company's work, the stage of consolidation of position in the company and industry, the mid-life crisis, or the stage of reflection on one's own destiny and the company's strategy (Lansberg, 1991).

An important contribution to research on the longevity of family businesses is made by the Cambridge Institute for Family Enterprise. This unit studies the development cycles of businesses and their owners' families in 30 countries over 17 generations (Davis et al., 2019). The literature notes examples of family businesses in which succession has occurred dozens of times. The oldest family businesses in the world are shown in Table 1.

Table 1. Oldest family businesses in the world

Name of the Company	Year of foundation	Country	Sector
Houshi Onsen Ryokan	718	Japan	Restaurant and hotels
Marchesi Antinori SRL	1358	Italy	Wine producer
Fabbrica d'Armi Pietro Beretta S.p.A.	1526	Italy	Firearms
John Brooke & Sons Ltd	1541	UK	Textile industry
Freiherr Von Poschinger Glasmanufaktur	1568	Germany	Glass craft

Name of the Company	Year of foundation	Country	Sector
R. Dunnett & Son	1591	UK	Construction industry
Mellerio dits Meller	1613	France	Jewerly
Avedis Zildjian Co.	1623	Turkey	Tableware manufacturing
Shirley Plantation	1638	USA	Agriculture and tourism
Hugel & Flis	1639	France	Wine producer
Van Eeghen International BV	1662	Northen Ireland	Maritime transportation
C. Hoare & Co.	1672	UK	Banking
William Clark & Sons	1739	Northen Ireland	Underwear
Boplaas	1743	South Africa	Agriculture
Bachman Funeral Home	1769	USA	Funeral home
Confetti Mario Pelino	1783	Italy	Confectionery production
Bixler's Jewelry	1785	USA	Jewerly store
Molson, Inc.	1786	Canada	Brewery
George R. Ruhl & Son, inc	1789	USA	Bakery

Source: Ł. Sułkowski and A. Marjański (2009). *Firmy rodzinne. Jak osiągnąć sukces w sztafecie pokoleń.* Warszawa: Poltext; W.T. O'Hara (2003). *Centuries of Success: Lessons from the World's Most Enduring Family Business.* Avon: Adam Media.

The average lifespan of a family business in Western countries is 60 years (Zellweger et al., 2012a), but in countries where a market economy has existed for a short time, such as Poland, this ratio is significantly lower (Wysocka, 2019). The largest number of long-lived family businesses is found in Japan. Approx. 100,000 companies there are over 100 years old. Nearly 100 Japanese companies have existed for over 600 years. The real estate trading company Kongo Gumi (founded in 578) is considered the oldest. In 2006, its last owner handed over the business to a construction group. Another example is the Houshi Onsen hotel and spa (in operation since 718), which is now managed by the 46th descendant of the founder. The oldest European family businesses are the Chateau de Gaulaine vineyard (Haute-Goulaine, France) and the Pontificia Fonderia Marinelli bell foundry (Agnone, Italy), established around the 1000. In Germany, the oldest family business is the Pilgrim Haus hotel (Soest, Westphalia, founded in 1304), in the UK – the John Brooke & Sons textile factory (Huddersfield, Yorkshire, founded in 1541) (Goto, 2014). Some of the oldest Polish family businesses include:

- The Baczewski distillery, launched in 1782 in Lviv, is world famous for its production of spirits. After World War II, it was launched in Vienna;
- Jan Felczynski Bell Foundary, the Felczynski Bell Foundry, founded in 1808 in Kalusz, Podolia; since 1948, the plant has operated in Przemyśl under the name Jan Felczynski Bell Foundry and Repair;
- W. Kruk jewellery company, founded in 1840 in Poznan. Its entry into the GWP in 2002 resulted in its acquisition by Vistula Group S.A. Capital Group;
- Blikle Confectionery. It has been operating in Warsaw since 1869. Recently, the plant has been in financial trouble because of a decline in demand for creamers and the admission of a new shareholder who understood the strategy of the family business in his own way;
- Warsaw workshops and artisans studios: The Workshop of Bronze Art Articles, Lopienski Brothers (in existence since 1862), the shoe-making workshop Jan Kielman and Son (1883), and the corsetry workshop "Aniela" (1896).

The ranking of the largest family businesses was compiled at the Department of Family Business at the University of St. Gallen. The list included the

500 largest enterprises, taking the company's income for the last 24 months as a criterion. The prerequisites for an entity to be considered a family business were the involvement of at least one family member on the board of directors and the family's share of the controlling stake of at least 32%. The list included companies from the following countries: the US 122 (24.4%), Germany 79 (15.8%), France 28 (5.6%), Hong Kong 20 (4%), and India and Switzerland 18 (3.6%). According to the data got, the revenue of the 500 largest family businesses increased by 9.9% between 2017 and 2019, while the revenue of Fortune 500 companies (where family businesses occupy less than half the seats) increased by 8.6%. This shows the ability of family businesses to compete in markets. Almost half of the 30 companies listed are at least 80 years old, including seven founded in the 19th century and only two after 2000. The list of the 500 largest family businesses for 2021 shows that 33% of these companies are over 100 years old, while 75% are over 50 years old. Nearly half of them operate in Europe (Robertson and Zellweger, 2019).

Table 2. Largest family businesses in the world

Company Name	Founders Family	Year of Founding	Revenue, bilion USD	Employment, thous. people	Sector	Country
Wal-Mart	Walton	1962	485,9	2300	discount stores	USA
Volkswagen AG	Porsche	1937	287,9	642	automotive industry	Germany
Berkshire Hathaway, Inc.	Buffet	1955	242,1	402	financial services	USA

Company Name	Founders Family	Year of Founding	Revenue, bilion USD	Employment, thous. people	Sector	Country
EXOR SpA	Agnelli	1927	170,8	310	financial services	Italy
Ford Motor Company	Ford	1903	156,8	202	automotive industry	USA
Bayerische Motoren Werke AG (BMW)	Quandt	1916	118,8	130	automotive industry	Germany
Koch Industries Inc.	Koch	1940	110,0	100	communications conglomerate	USA
Cargill, Incorporated	Cargill	1865	109,7	153	consumer goods	USA
Schwarz Group	Schwarz	1930	109,6	360	consumer goods	Germany
Robert Bosch GmbH	Bosch	1886	94,6	400	auto parts	Germany
ALDI Group	Albrecht	1913	84,9	170	retail	Germany
Comcast Corp.	Roberts	1963	84,5	164	telecommunications, media	USA

Company Name	Founders Family	Year of Founding	Revenue, bilion USD	Employment, thous. people	Sector	Country
Arcelor Mittal	Mittal	1975	68,7	197	power industry, metallurgy	Luxembourg
Gunvor SA	Törnqvist	2000	64,0	2	power industry	Switzerland
Dell Technologies Inc.	Dell	1984	61,6	138	telecommunications, media	USA
Metro AG	Haniel, Schmidt, Beisheim	1996	60,2	60	modern infrastructure	Germany
Roche Holding AG	Hoffman and Oeri	1896	56,5	100	health and welfare services	Switzerland
LG Corporation	Koo and He	1947	55,7	130	telecommunications, media	South Korea
Continental AG	Schaeffler	1871	53,2	235	communications conglomerate	Germany
Groupe 3 SA	Mulliez	1961	53,1	355	retail	France

Source: Ł. Sułkowski and A. Marjański (2009). *Firmy rodzinne. Jak osiągnąć sukces w sztafecie pokoleń.* Warszawa: Poltext; H. Robertsson and T. Zellweger (2019). *The Global Family Business Index.* St. Gallen: University of St. Gallen.

It is worth citing in conclusion the results of a survey of 2,500 representatives of family businesses from around the world (KPMG, 2021). They confirmed the opinion of the "unique strength of family businesses." The report enumerates the following factors for the success and sustainability of family businesses:

- The ambition and enthusiasm of the company's founder, if he or she transfers this to the next generation.
- Entrepreneurial orientation as a mix of innovation, activity and willingness to take risks.
- Investment in research and development, creation of new products and digitization;
- Family unity and engaging the next generation in business.
- A holistic view of company performance. Taking into account not only profitability, but also customer loyalty and a good reputation.
- Not autocratic, but transactional or charismatic leadership that inspires and motivates employees and other stakeholders.
- Supplementing the resources of the family business with social-emotional wealth.

Effective succession, company longevity and sustainable development

The above factors of success and longevity of family businesses are often referred to by social activists and politicians. However, the literature often points to the weak presence of these factors in the daily practice of family businesses. A paper presenting the opinions of a wide range of practitioners speaks for the development of a specific organizational culture and social responsibility of family businesses.

Succession and the longevity of a family business can raise some psychological barriers. This is because it is related to the generational change, and in a broader perspective – to the drama of human passing, which not every entrepreneur likes to discuss. However, this does not change the fact that longevity represents a certain value that cannot be converted into financial acquires. Entrepreneurs who have successfully gone through succession see a more fundamental value in the longevity of their company. According to I. Walkowska (president of PLASTWIL, a plastics processing plant), who went through a successful succession, "family businesses are often characterized by the great faith and above-average commitment of the founders and their successors to the development and success of the company. For its partners and counterparties, a multigenerational family business often signifies the stability of its operation and the sustainability of the values under which the company operates" (PWC 2016).

The advantage of family businesses is the long-term orientation of business activity and the desire to pass the business on to descendants, i.e., towards longevity and continuity of development. In the functioning of such an enterprise, "family logic" often dominates over "business logic", family values over economic values. Such properties of family enterprises are closely correlated with the concept of balanced and lasting socio-economic development, which is widely promoted today. Although the latter refers rather to the economy, the role of family enterprises, both in implementing and benefiting from the effects of this idea, is fundamental. It can even be said that family businesses are becoming an important factor in sustainable development.

References

Bar J. (2018). *Nestor i sukcesor. Model zarządzania firmą rodzinną z uwzględnieniem jej cyklu życia*. Warszawa: Biblioteka Sulisław.

Cipiur J. (2019). *Najstarsze przedsiębiorstwa w biznesie*. Studio Opinii – portal.

Davis J., Cohen J., Jay I. and Runner J. (2019). *Future Family Enterprise: Sustaining Multigenerational Success*. Cambridge, MA: Cambridge Institute for Family Enterprise.

Deloitte (2016). *Nowe pokolenie w firmach rodzinnych. Rozwój i zachowanie rodzinnych wartości*. Warszawa: Deloitte.

Dźwigoł-Barosz M. (2017). *Kształtowanie kompetencji z obszaru inteligencji emocjonalnej w procesie sukcesji współczesnych przedsiębiorstw rodzinnych*. Warszawa: Wydawnictwo Naukowe PWN.

European Commission (1994). "Commission Recommendation of 7 December 1994 on the transfer of small and medium-sized enterprises". https://eur-lex.europa.eu/legal-content/HU/TXT/?uri=CELEX:31994H1069. Accessed: 19.12.2023.

European Commission (2003). "Helping the transfer of business. A 'good practice guide' of measures for supporting the transfer of business to new ownership". Bruxelles: European Commission.

European Commission (2009). "Overview of Family-Business-Relevant Issues: Research, Networks, Policy Measures and Existing Studies". https://ec.europa.eu/docsroom/documents/10388/attachments/1/translations/en/renditions/native. Accessed: 19.12.2023.

Family Business (2023). "Europejski Kongres Gospodarczy – Relacja z panelu o sukcesji moderowanego przez Instytut Biznesu Rodzinnego". https://familybusiness.ibrpolska.pl/europejski-kongres-gospodarczy-relacja-z-panelu-o-sukcesji-moderowanego-przez-instytut-biznesu-rodzinnego. Accessed: 19.12.2023.

Family Business Yearbook (2015). London: Ernest & Young Publishing.

Goto T. (2014). "Family business and its longevity". *Kindai Management Review* 2, 78–96.

Hutcheson H. (2022). *Dirty Little Secrets of Family Business: Ensuring Success from One Generation to the Next.* Austin: Greenleaf Book Group Press.

Jeżak J. (ed.). (2014). *Przedsiębiorstwa rodzinne w Polsce.* Łódź: Wydawnictwo Uniwersytetu Łódzkiego.

KPMG (2020). "Barometr firm rodzinnych. Edycja 2020. W stronę wielopokoleniowości". https://assets.kpmg.com/content/dam/kpmg/pl/pdf/2020/02/pl-raport-kpmg-barometr-firm-rodzinnych-edycja-osma.pdf. Accessed: 19.12.2023.

KPMG (2021). *Mastering a comeback. How family businesses are triumphing over Covid-19.* Retrieved from https://kpmg.com/xx/en/home/insights/2021/02/global-family-business-report-covid-19-edition.html. Accessed: 19.12.2023.

Kuta K., Matejun M. and Miksa P. (2017). "Długowieczność firm rodzinnych". *Przegląd Nauk Ekonomicznych* 26, 91–102.

Lansberg I. (1991). "On retirement: A conversation with Daniel Levinson". *Family Business Review* 3(1), 59–73. https://doi.org/10.1111/j.1741-6248.1991.00059.x

Leach P. (2017). *Firmy rodzinne. Wszystko, co istotne.* Warszawa: Deloitte, Studio EMKA.

Lewandowska A. (2015). *Kody wartości. Czyli jak efektywnie przejść przez sukcesję w firmie rodzinnej.* Poznań: Instytut Biznesu Rodzinnego.

Lewandowska A. (2021). *Strategiczna logika firm rodzinnych.* Warszawa: Wydawnictwo Naukowe PWN, IBR.

Lewandowska A. and Lipiec J. (2015). *Konstytucje firm rodzinnych: w kierunku długowieczności*. Warszawa: Wolters Kluwer.

Lewandowska A. and Lipiec J. (2021). *Konstytucja rodzinna. Zasady rodziny i biznesu prowadzące do długowieczności*. Warszawa: Wydawnictwo Naukowe PWN, IBR.

Lewandowska A., Martyniec Ł. and Adamska M. (2015). *Przewodnik SOS. Sytuacja nagłej sukcesji*. Warszawa: PARP.

Małyszek E. (2011). "Czynniki wpływające na sukces i długoterminowe przetrwanie firm rodzinnych". *Przedsiębiorczość i Zarządzanie* 7, 82–96.

Marjański A. (ed.). (2016). *Sukcesja biznesu, czyli jak zadbać o bezpieczeństwo przedsiębiorstwa i rodziny*. Gdańsk: ODDK.

May P. and Lewandowska A. (2021). *Stawka większa niż biznes. Droga rozwoju firmy rodzinnej i rodziny biznesowej*. Warszawa: Wydawnictwo Naukowe PWN, IBR.

Ministerstwo Przedsiębiorczości i Technologii (2019). *Fundacja rodzinna Zielona Księga*. Warszawa.

Ministerstwo Rozwoju i Technologii. (2023). *Sukcesja firm*. www.gov.pl/web/rozwoj-technologia/sukcesja-firm. Accessed: 19.12.2023.

O'Hara W.T. (2003). *Centuries of Success: Lessons from the World's Most Enduring Family Business*. Avon: Adam Media.

PARP (2014). *Przewodnik po sukcesji w firmach rodzinnych*. Kraków: PARP.

PARP (2016). *Diagnoza sytuacji sukcesyjnej w przedsiębiorstwach rodzinnych w Polsce. Syntetyczny raport z badań w ramach projektu „Kody wartości"*. Warszawa: PARP.

Piekarski W. and Rudzińska J. (2012). "Znaczenie sukcesji w polskich firmach rodzinnych". *Logistyka* 4, 1200–1205.

PWC (2016). *Udana sukcesja podstawą dynamicznego rozwoju*. www.pwc.pl/pl/publikacje/2016/badanie-firm-rodzinnych-2016/izabella-walkowska-prezes-firmy-plastwil.html. Accessed: 19.12.2023.

Ramadani V., Memili E., Palalić R. and Chang E.P.C. (2020). *Entrepreneurial Family Businesses Innovation, Governance, and Succession*. Springer Nature Switzerland AG. https://doi.org/10.1007/978-3-030-47778-3.

Robertsson H. and Zellweger T. (2019). *The Global Family Business Index*. St. Gallen: University of St. Gallen.

Romanowska E. (2017). *Przedsiębiorczość rodzinna i jej sukcesja*. Warszawa: PARP.

Rothwell W.J. and Prescott R.K. (2023). *Succession Planning for Small and Family Businesses: Navigating Successful Transitions*. London: Routledge.

Sejm RP (2017). Ustawa z dnia 27 października 2017 r. o zmianie ustawy o podatku dochodowym od osób fizycznych, ustawy o podatku dochodowym od osób prawnych oraz ustawy o zryczałtowanym podatku dochodowym od niektórych przychodów osiąganych przez osoby fizyczne, Dz.U. z 2017 r., poz. 2175.

Sejm RP. (2018). Ustawa z dnia 5 lipca 2018 r. o zarządzie sukcesyjnych przedsiębiorstwa osoby fizycznej, Dz.U. z 2018 r., poz. 1629.

Sejm RP. (2023). Ustawa z dnia 26 stycznia 2023 r. o fundacji rodzinnej, Dz.U. z 2023 r., poz. 326.

Sułkowski Ł. and Marjański A. (2009). *Firmy rodzinne. Jak osiągnąć sukces w sztafecie pokoleń*. Warszawa: Poltext.

Sułkowski Ł. and Marjański A. (2019). *Firmy rodzinne – problemy poznawcze*. Łódź: Społeczna Akademia Nauk.

Surdej A. and Wach K. (2010). *Przedsiębiorstwa rodzinne wobec wyzwań sukcesji*. Warszawa: Difin.

Thier A. (2020). "The importance and consolidation of family businesses in the contemporary economy". *Zeszyty Naukowe Uniwersytetu Ekonomicznego w Krakowie* 6(990), 7–27.

Thinktank (2018). "Rodzina, majątek, firma: rozmowy o udanej sukcesji". https://ssw. solutions/app/uploads/2018/04/THINKTANK_Sukcesja_PUBLIKACJA. pdf. Accessed: 19.12.2023.

Urząd Marszałkowski w Krakowie (2023). "Plan zarządzania sukcesją w Małopolsce 2030". Kraków.

Ward J.L. (2004). *Perpetuating the Family Business*. New York: Palgrave Macmillan.

Więcek-Janka E. (2013). "Firmy rodzinne – przedsiębiorczość długowieczna". *Przedsiębiorczość i Zarządzanie* 3, 259–274.

Wojewoda M. (2019). *Skutki sukcesji w firmie rodzinnej*. Poznań: IBR.

Wysocka M. (2019). "Determinanty sprawnego działania przedsiębiorstw rodzinnych w Hiszpanii, Polsce, Turcji oraz na Łotwie". *Forum Teologiczne* 20, 61–73.

Yuan X.H. (2019). "A review of succession and innovation in family business". *American Journal of Industries and Business Management* 9, 974–990. https://doi. org/10.4236/ajibm.2019.94066.

Zellweger T.M., Kellermanns F.W., Chrisman J.J. and Chua J.H. (2012a). "Family control and family firm valuation by family CEOs: The importance of intentions for transgenerational control". *Organization Science* 23(3), 851–868.

Zellweger T.M., Nason R.S. and Nordqvist M. (2012b). "From longevity of firms to transgenerational entrepreneurship of families". *Family Business Review* 2, 136–155. https://doi.org/10.1177/0894486511423531.

Copy editor
Jolanta Grzegorzek

Language editors
Renata Włodek
Katarzyna Zajdel

Proofreader
Klaudia Król-Kiełbowicz

Typesetter
Paweł Noszkiewicz

Jagiellonian University Press
Editorial Offices: ul. Michałowskiego 9/2, 31-126 Krakow
Phone: +48 12 663 23 80

Printed in the USA
CPSIA information can be obtained
at www.ICGtesting.com
JSHW011442051024
71096JS00011B/98